MARK

The Humanity of Christ

JOHN MACARTHUR

THOMAS NELSON
Since 1798

MARK
MACARTHUR BIBLE STUDIES

Published in Nashville, Tennessee, by Nelson Books, an imprint of Thomas Nelson. Nelson Books and Thomas Nelson are registered trademarks of HarperCollins Christian Publishing, Inc.

Nelson Books titles may be purchased in bulk for education, business, fundraising, or sales promotional use. For information, please email SpecialMarkets@ThomasNelson.com

Published in association with the literary agency of Wolgemuth & Associates, Inc.

Produced with the assistance of the Livingstone Corporation. Project staff include Jake Barton, Betsy Todt Schmitt, and Andy Culbertson.

Project editors: Mary Horner Collins, Amber Rae, and Len Woods

Cover Art by Holly Sharp Design
Interior Design and Composition by Joel Bartlett, Livingstone Corporation

ISBN: 978-0-7180-3502-0

Printed in the United States of America.
HB 05.30.2024

CONTENTS

INTRODUCTION TO MARK

Mark, for whom this Gospel is named, was a close companion of the apostle Peter and a recurring character in the book of Acts, where he is known as "John whose surname was Mark" (Acts 12:12, 25; 15:37, 39). It was to John Mark's mother's home in Jerusalem that Peter went when released from prison (Acts 12:12).

John Mark was a cousin of Barnabas (Col. 4:10), who accompanied Paul and Barnabas on Paul's first missionary journey (Acts 12:25–13:5). But he left them at Perga and returned to Jerusalem (Acts 13:13). When Barnabas wanted Paul to take John Mark on the second missionary journey, Paul refused. The resulting friction between Paul and Barnabas led to their separation (Acts 15:38–40).

John Mark's earlier vacillation, however, evidently gave way to strength and maturity, and in time he proved himself even to the apostle Paul. When Paul wrote the Colossians, he instructed them that if John Mark were to come, they were to welcome him (Col. 4:10). Paul even listed Mark as a fellow worker (Philem. 24). Later, Paul told Timothy, "Get Mark and bring him with you, for he is useful to me for ministry" (2 Tim. 4:11).

John Mark's restoration to useful ministry may have been, in part, due to the ministry of Peter. Peter's close relationship with Mark is evident from his description of him as "Mark my son" (1 Pet. 5:13). Peter, of course, was no stranger to failure himself, and his influence on the younger man was, no doubt, instrumental in helping him out of the instability of his youth and into the strength and maturity he would need for the work to which God had called him.

AUTHOR AND DATE

Unlike the Epistles, the Gospels do not name their authors in their texts. The early church fathers, however, unanimously affirm that Mark wrote this second Gospel. Papias, bishop of Hieropolis, writing about AD 140, noted: "And the presbyter [the apostle John] said this: 'Mark having become the interpreter of Peter, wrote down accurately whatsoever he remembered. It was not, however, in exact order that he related the sayings or deeds of Christ. For he neither heard the Lord nor accompanied Him. But afterwards, as I said, he accompanied Peter, who accommodated his instructions to the necessities [of his hearers], but with no intention of giving a regular narrative of the Lord's sayings. Wherefore Mark made no mistake in thus writing some things as he remembered them. For one thing he took special care not to omit anything he had heard and not to put anything fictitious into the statements.' " [From the *Exposition of the Oracles of the Lord* (6)]

Justin Martyr, writing about AD 150, referred to the Gospel of Mark as "the memoirs of Peter," and suggested that Mark wrote his Gospel in Italy. This agrees with the uniform voice of early tradition, which regarded this Gospel as having been written in Rome for the benefit of Roman Christians. Writing about AD 185, Irenaeus called Mark "the disciple and interpreter of Peter," and he noted that the second Gospel consists of what Peter preached about Christ. The testimony of the church fathers differs as to whether this Gospel was written before or after Peter's death (ca. AD 67–68).

Evangelical scholars have suggested dates for the writing of Mark's Gospel ranging from AD 50 to 70. A date before the destruction of Jerusalem and the Temple in AD 70 is required by Jesus' comment recorded in 13:2, referring to the Temple: "Do you see these great buildings? Not one stone shall be left upon another, that shall not be thrown down."

Luke's Gospel was clearly written before Acts (Acts 1:1–3). The date of the writing of Acts can probably be fixed around AD 63 because that is shortly after the narrative ends. It is likely, therefore, though not certain, that Mark was written at an early date, sometime in the 50s.

BACKGROUND AND SETTING

While Matthew was written to a Jewish audience, Mark seems to have targeted Roman believers, particularly Gentiles. When employing Aramaic terms, Mark translated them for his readers (3:17; 5:41; 7:11, 34; 10:46; 14:36; 15:22, 34). On the other hand, in some places he used Latin expressions instead of their Greek equivalents (5:9; 12:15, 42; 15:16, 39). He also reckoned time according to the Roman system (6:48; 13:35) and carefully explained Jewish customs (7:3–4; 14:12; 15:42). Mark omitted Jewish elements, such as the genealogies found in Matthew and Luke. This Gospel also makes fewer references to the Old Testament and includes less material that would be of particular interest to Jewish readers, such as that which is critical of the Pharisees and Sadducees (Sadducees are mentioned only once, in 12:18). When mentioning Simon the Cyrene (15:21), Mark identifies him as the father of Rufus, a prominent member of the church at Rome (Rom. 16:13). All of this supports the traditional view that Mark was written for a Gentile audience initially at Rome.

Historical and Theological Themes

Mark presents Jesus as the suffering Servant of the Lord (10:45). His focus is on the deeds of Jesus more than His teaching, particularly emphasizing service and sacrifice. Mark omits the lengthy discourses found in the other Gospels, often relating only brief excerpts to give the gist of Jesus' teaching. Mark also omits any account of Jesus' ancestry and birth, beginning where Jesus' public ministry began with His baptism by John in the wilderness.

Mark demonstrates the humanity of Christ more clearly than any of the other evangelists, emphasizing Christ's human emotions (1:41; 3:5; 6:34; 8:12; 9:36), His human limitations (4:38; 11:12; 13:32), and other small details that highlight the human side of the Son of God (for example, 7:33–34; 8:12; 9:36; 10:13–16).

Interpretive Challenges

Three significant questions confront the interpreter of Mark:

1. What is the relationship of Mark to Luke and Matthew? (see below, "*The Synoptic Problem*")
2. How should one interpret the eschatological passages?
3. Are the last twelve verses of chapter 16 originally part of Mark's Gospel?

The Synoptic Problem

Even a cursory reading of Matthew, Mark, and Luke reveals both striking similarities (2:3–12; Matt. 9:2–8; Luke 5:18–26) and significant differences, as each views the life, ministry, and teaching of Jesus. The question of how to explain those similarities and differences is known as the "Synoptic Problem" (*syn* means "together"; *optic* means "seeing").

The modern solution—even among some evangelicals—has been to assume that some form or literary dependence exists among the synoptic Gospels. The most commonly accepted theory to explain such an alleged literary dependence is known as the "Two-Source" theory. According to that hypothesis, Mark was the first Gospel written, and Matthew and Luke then used Mark as a source in writing their Gospels.

Proponents of this view imagine a non-existent second source, labeled Q (from the German word *Quelle*, "source"), and argue that this is the source of the material in Matthew and Luke that does not appear in Mark. They advance several lines of evidence to support their scenario.

First, most of Mark is paralleled in Matthew and Luke. Since it is much shorter than Matthew and Luke, the latter must be expansions of Mark.

Second, the three Gospels follow the same general chronological outline; but when either Matthew or Luke departs from Mark's chronology, the other agrees with Mark. Put another way, Matthew and Luke do not both depart from Mark's chronology in the same places. That, it is argued, shows that Matthew and Luke used Mark for their historical framework.

Third, in passages common to all three Gospels, Matthew's and Luke's wording seldom agrees when they differ from Mark's. Proponents of the "Two-Source" theory see this as confirmation that Matthew and Luke used Mark's Gospel as a source.

Those arguments do not prove that Matthew and Luke used Mark's Gospel as a source, however. In fact, the weight of evidence is strongly against such a theory:

1. The nearly unanimous testimony of the church until the nineteenth century was that Matthew was the first Gospel written. Such an impressive body of evidence cannot be ignored.

2. Why would Matthew, an apostle and eyewitness to the events of Christ's life, depend on Mark (who was not an eyewitness)—even for the account of his own conversion?

3. A significant statistical analysis of the synoptic Gospels has revealed that the parallels between them are far less extensive and the differences more significant than is commonly acknowledged. The differences, in particular, argue against literary dependence among the Gospel writers.

4. Since the Gospels record actual historical events, it would be surprising if they did not follow the same general historical sequence. For example, the fact that three books on American history all have the Revolutionary War, the Civil War, World War I, World War II, the Vietnam War, and the Gulf War in the same chronological order would not prove that the authors had read each others' books. General agreement in content does not prove literary dependency.

5. The passages in which Matthew and Luke agree against Mark (see argument 3 in favor of the "Two-Source" theory) amount to about one-sixth of Matthew and one-sixth of Luke. If they used Mark's Gospel as a source, there is no satisfactory explanation for why Matthew and Luke would so often both change Mark's wording in the same way.

6. The "Two-Source" theory cannot account for the important section in Mark's Gospel (6:45–8:26) that Luke omits. This omission suggests Luke had not seen Mark's Gospel when he wrote his book.

7. There is no historical or manuscript evidence that the Q document ever existed; it is purely a fabrication of modern skepticism and a way to possibly deny the verbal inspiration of the Gospels.

8. Any theory of literary dependence between Gospel writers overlooks the significance of their personal contacts with each other. Mark and Luke were both companions of Paul (Philem. 24); the early church (including Matthew) met for a time in the home of Mark's mother (Acts 12:12); and Luke could easily have met Matthew during Paul's two-year imprisonment at Caesarea. Such contacts make theories of mutual literary dependence unnecessary.

The simplest solution to the Synoptic Problem is that no such problem exists! Because critics cannot prove literary dependence among the Gospel writers, there is no need to explain it. The traditional view that the Gospel writers were inspired by God and wrote independently of each other—except that all three were moved by the same Holy Spirit (2 Pet. 1:20)—remains the only plausible view.

As the reader compares the various viewpoints in the Gospels, it becomes clear how well they harmonize and lead to a more complete picture of the whole event or message. The accounts are not contradictory but complementary, revealing a fuller understanding when brought together.

NOTES

1

INAUGURATING THE SERVANT
Mark 1:1-2:28

DRAWING NEAR

How and when did you hear the good news about Jesus? What were your
first impressions of Him?

_____

_____

_____

THE CONTEXT

Mark's Gospel was intended for a Gentile audience, especially a Roman one.
Mark is the Gospel of action; the frequent use of "immediately" and "then" keeps
his narrative moving rapidly along. Jesus appears in Mark as the Servant (Mark
10:45) who bursts on the scene to suffer for the sins of many. Mark's fast-paced
approach would especially appeal to the practical, action-oriented Romans.

Without commenting on Christ's birth or childhood, Mark begins his record
of the life of Jesus with a description of John the Baptist—the one prophesied
to be the forerunner of Messiah. The brief public ministry of John the Baptist
paved the way for the introduction and inauguration of God's Servant (1:1–11).
Mark then quickly sketches the beginning of Christ's ministry—His temptation
and His departure from Judea (due to opposition at home). Relocating his
headquarters in Galilee, Jesus set about calling some disciples, teaching in the
synagogue of Capernaum (authenticated by the healing of a demoniac), healing
many (including Peter's mother-in-law), touring Galilee with Simon and others,
and cleansing a leper followed by much (unwelcome) publicity. Chapter two of
Mark continues this rapid-fire description of events—forgiving and healing a
paralytic, calling Matthew, and attending the banquet at Matthew's house.

Next, Mark sets the stage for what is to come as he describes the beginning
of controversies with the Jewish leaders over the Sabbath—beginning with the
incident involving the disciples' picking grain on the day of rest.

KEYS TO THE TEXT

Gospel: The Greek word translated as _gospel_ means "a reward for bringing
good news" or simply "good news." In His famous sermon at the synagogue in

Nazareth, Jesus quoted Isaiah 61:1 to characterize the spirit of His ministry: "The Spirit of the Lord is upon Me, because He has anointed Me to preach the gospel [good news] to the poor" (Luke 4:18). The gospel is not a new plan of salvation; it is the fulfillment of God's plan of salvation that was begun through the nation of Israel, was completed in Jesus Christ, and is made known by the church. The gospel is the saving work of God in His Son Jesus Christ and a call to faith in Him. Jesus is more than a messenger of the gospel; He *is* the gospel. The good news of God was present in His life, teaching, and atoning death. Therefore, the gospel is both a historical event and a personal relationship. (*Nelson's New Illustrated Bible Dictionary*)

UNLEASHING THE TEXT

Read 1:1–2:28, noting the key words and definitions next to the passage.

gospel (v. 1)—the good news about the life, death, and resurrection of Jesus Christ

Jesus Christ (v. 1)—"Jesus" is the Greek form of the Hebrew name *Joshua* ("the Lord is salvation"); "Christ" signifies His office as ruler of God's coming kingdom.

baptizing (v. 4)—John's baptism was different from the Jewish washing rituals in that it was a one-time act symbolizing the need to come to God through repentance and faith.

baptism of repentance (v. 4)—a baptism resulting from true repentance (that is, a turning from sin to God, resulting in righteous living)

confessing their sins (v. 5)—agreeing with God about them

baptize you with the Holy Spirit (v. 8)—This takes place when a person comes to faith in Christ.

Nazareth (v. 9)—an obscure village 70 miles north of Jerusalem, not mentioned in the Old Testament

Mark 1:1–2:28 (NKJV)

1 *The beginning of the gospel of Jesus Christ, the Son of God.*

2 *As it is written in the Prophets: "Behold, I send My messenger before Your face, Who will prepare Your way before You."*

3 *"The voice of one crying in the wilderness: 'Prepare the way of the Lord; Make His paths straight.'"*

4 *John came baptizing in the wilderness and preaching a baptism of repentance for the remission of sins.*

5 *Then all the land of Judea, and those from Jerusalem, went out to him and were all baptized by him in the Jordan River, confessing their sins.*

6 *Now John was clothed with camel's hair and with a leather belt around his waist, and he ate locusts and wild honey.*

7 *And he preached, saying, "There comes One after me who is mightier than I, whose sandal strap I am not worthy to stoop down and loose.*

8 *I indeed baptized you with water, but He will baptize you with the Holy Spirit."*

9 *It came to pass in those days that Jesus came from Nazareth of Galilee, and was baptized by John in the Jordan.*

10 *And immediately, coming up from the water, He saw the heavens parting and the Spirit descending upon Him like a dove.*

11 *Then a voice came from heaven, "You are My beloved Son, in whom I am well pleased."*

12 *Immediately the Spirit drove Him into the wilderness.*

13 *And He was there in the wilderness forty days, tempted by Satan, and was with the wild beasts; and the angels ministered to Him.*

14 *Now after John was put in prison, Jesus came to Galilee, preaching the gospel of the kingdom of God,*

15 *and saying, "The time is fulfilled, and the kingdom of God is at hand. Repent, and believe in the gospel."*

16 *And as He walked by the Sea of Galilee, He saw Simon and Andrew his brother casting a net into the sea; for they were fishermen.*

17 *Then Jesus said to them, "Follow Me, and I will make you become fishers of men."*

18 *They immediately left their nets and followed Him.*

19 *When He had gone a little farther from there, He saw James the son of Zebedee, and John his brother, who also were in the boat mending their nets.*

20 *And immediately He called them, and they left their father Zebedee in the boat with the hired servants, and went after Him.*

21 *Then they went into Capernaum, and immediately on the Sabbath He entered the synagogue and taught.*

22 *And they were astonished at His teaching, for He taught them as one having authority, and not as the scribes.*

23 *Now there was a man in their synagogue with an unclean spirit. And he cried out,*

24 *saying, "Let us alone! What have we to do with You, Jesus of Nazareth? Did You come to destroy us? I know who You are—the Holy One of God!"*

25 *But Jesus rebuked him, saying, "Be quiet, and come out of him!"*

the Spirit descending upon Him like a dove (v. 10)—most likely a symbol of Jesus' empowerment for ministry

the Spirit drove Him (v. 12)—Jesus was compelled by the Spirit to confront Satan and take the first step in overthrowing his evil kingdom.

John was put in prison (v. 14)—Herod incarcerated John because John had rebuked Herod's incestuous relationship with Herodias, Herod's neice.

the kingdom of God is at hand (v. 15)—because the King was present

fishers of men (v. 17)—Evangelism was the primary purpose for which Jesus called the apostles.

synagogue (v. 21)—literally, "to gather together"; the place where Jewish people gathered for worship

authority (v. 22)—Jesus' direct, personal, and forceful teaching was in sharp contrast to the scribes, who mainly quoted other rabbis.

the Holy One of God (v. 24)—a demonic affirmation of Jesus' sinlessness and deity

Simon's wife's mother (v. 30)—
Peter was married.

26 *And when the unclean spirit had convulsed him and cried out with a loud voice, he came out of him.*

27 *Then they were all amazed, so that they questioned among themselves, saying, "What is this? What new doctrine is this? For with authority He commands even the unclean spirits, and they obey Him."*

28 *And immediately His fame spread throughout all the region around Galilee.*

29 *Now as soon as they had come out of the synagogue, they entered the house of Simon and Andrew, with James and John.*

30 *But Simon's wife's mother lay sick with a fever, and they told Him about her at once.*

31 *So He came and took her by the hand and lifted her up, and immediately the fever left her. And she served them.*

32 *At evening, when the sun had set, they brought to Him all who were sick and those who were demon-possessed.*

33 *And the whole city was gathered together at the door.*

34 *Then He healed many who were sick with various diseases, and cast out many demons; and He did not allow the demons to speak, because they knew Him.*

35 *Now in the morning, having risen a long while before daylight, He went out and departed to a solitary place; and there He prayed.*

36 *And Simon and those who were with Him searched for Him.*

37 *When they found Him, they said to Him, "Everyone is looking for You."*

38 *But He said to them, "Let us go into the next towns, that I may preach there also, because for this purpose I have come forth."*

39 *And He was preaching in their synagogues throughout all Galilee, and casting out demons.*

40 *Now a leper came to Him, imploring Him, kneeling down to Him and saying to Him, "If You are willing, You can make me clean."*

41 *Then Jesus, moved with compassion, stretched out His hand and touched him, and said to him, "I am willing; be cleansed."*

42 *As soon as He had spoken, immediately the leprosy left him, and he was cleansed.*

43 *And He strictly warned him and sent him away at once,*

44 *and said to him, "See that you say nothing to anyone; but go your way, show yourself to the priest, and offer for your cleansing those things which Moses commanded, as a testimony to them."*

45 *However, he went out and began to proclaim it freely, and to spread the matter, so that Jesus could no longer openly enter the city, but was outside in deserted places; and they came to Him from every direction.*

2:1 *And again He entered Capernaum after some days, and it was heard that He was in the house.*

2 *Immediately many gathered together, so that there was no longer room to receive them, not even near the door. And He preached the word to them.*

3 *Then they came to Him, bringing a paralytic who was carried by four men.*

4 *And when they could not come near Him because of the crowd, they uncovered the roof where He was. So when they had broken through, they let down the bed on which the paralytic was lying.*

5 *When Jesus saw their faith, He said to the paralytic, "Son, your sins are forgiven you."*

6 *And some of the scribes were sitting there and reasoning in their hearts,*

7 *"Why does this Man speak blasphemies like this? Who can forgive sins but God alone?"*

8 *But immediately, when Jesus perceived in His spirit that they reasoned thus within themselves, He said to them, "Why do you reason about these things in your hearts?*

9 *Which is easier, to say to the paralytic, 'Your sins are forgiven you,' or to say, 'Arise, take up your bed and walk'?*

touched him (v. 41)—Unlike rabbis, who avoided lepers lest they become ceremonially defiled, Jesus expressed compassion with a physical gesture.

say nothing to anyone (v. 44)—The ensuing publicity would hinder Jesus' ability to minister and divert attention away from His message.

they uncovered the roof (2:4)—That is, they dug through the clay, and then removed enough tiles or slabs on the flat roof to give them room to lower their sick friend directly in front of Jesus.

Which is easier (v. 9)—Obviously it is easier to say "Your sins are forgiven," since no human can prove that such an invisible thing has occurred.

tax office (v. 14)—Matthew was a publican or tax collector, and thus despised in Palestine because his job consisted of collecting revenues from his country-men and turning them over to the hated Romans; over-collecting was common and thus increased resentment towards publicans.

sinners (v. 15)—a term used by the Jews to refer to people who had no respect for the Mosaic law or rabbinical traditions

fasting (v. 18)—The twice-a-week fast was a major expression of orthodox Judaism during Jesus' day.

taken away from them (v. 20)—a sudden removal or violent snatching away; that is, a reference to Christ's capture and crucifixion

10 But that you may know that the Son of Man has power on earth to forgive sins"—He said to the paralytic,

11 "I say to you, arise, take up your bed, and go to your house."

12 Immediately he arose, took up the bed, and went out in the presence of them all, so that all were amazed and glorified God, saying, "We never saw anything like this!"

13 Then He went out again by the sea; and all the multitude came to Him, and He taught them.

14 As He passed by, He saw Levi the son of Alphaeus sitting at the tax office. And He said to him, "Follow Me." So he arose and followed Him.

15 Now it happened, as He was dining in Levi's house, that many tax collectors and sinners also sat together with Jesus and His disciples; for there were many, and they followed Him.

16 And when the scribes and Pharisees saw Him eating with the tax collectors and sinners, they said to His disciples, "How is it that He eats and drinks with tax collectors and sinners?"

17 When Jesus heard it, He said to them, "Those who are well have no need of a physician, but those who are sick. I did not come to call the righteous, but sinners, to repentance."

18 The disciples of John and of the Pharisees were fasting. Then they came and said to Him, "Why do the disciples of John and of the Pharisees fast, but Your disciples do not fast?"

19 And Jesus said to them, "Can the friends of the bridegroom fast while the bridegroom is with them? As long as they have the bridegroom with them they cannot fast.

20 But the days will come when the bridegroom will be taken away from them, and then they will fast in those days.

21 No one sews a piece of unshrunk cloth on an old garment; or else the new piece pulls away from the old, and the tear is made worse.

22 *And no one puts new wine into old wineskins; or else the new wine bursts the wineskins, the wine is spilled, and the wineskins are ruined. But new wine must be put into new wineskins."*

23 *Now it happened that He went through the grainfields on the Sabbath; and as they went His disciples began to pluck the heads of grain.*

24 *And the Pharisees said to Him, "Look, why do they do what is not lawful on the Sabbath?"*

25 *But He said to them, "Have you never read what David did when he was in need and hungry, he and those with him:*

26 *how he went into the house of God in the days of Abiathar the high priest, and ate the showbread, which is not lawful to eat except for the priests, and also gave some to those who were with him?"*

27 *And He said to them, "The Sabbath was made for man, and not man for the Sabbath.*

28 *Therefore the Son of Man is also Lord of the Sabbath."*

what is not lawful on the Sabbath (v. 24)—Legalistic rabbis had wrongly interpreted the rubbing of grain in the hands as a form of threshing, thus a kind of labor, forbidden on the day of rest.

Have you never read (v. 25)—a stinging remark pointing out the ignorance of those who took pride in their knowledge of Israel's law and history, and yet missed the deeper meaning

the showbread (v. 26)—twelve loaves of unleavened bread (representing the twelve tribes of Israel) that were placed on the table in the sanctuary and replaced each week

1) What was the role of John the Baptist, and why was it significant in the inauguration of Jesus' ministry?

_____

_____

_____

_____

(Verses to consider: Isa. 40:3; Mal. 3:1; Matt. 3:1–11; John 1:19–34)

2) Underline all the times Mark uses the word "immediately" in 1:1–2:28. What do you think Mark was trying to convey about Jesus and His ministry by using this term repeatedly?

_____

_____

_____

_____

3) Review the events that happened during the temptation of Christ in the wilderness. Identify three lessons you can learn from Jesus' example in dealing with Satan.

_____

_____

_____

_____

(Verses to consider: Matt. 4:1–11; Luke 4:1–13; Heb. 4:14–16; 1 John 3:8)

4) What miracles did Jesus do at the outset of His ministry, and what did they indicate or prove?

_____

_____

_____

Going Deeper

For a broader picture of Jesus' purpose, read Isaiah 52:13–53:3. This Old Testament passage provides some insight into what the coming Servant would do and experience.

Exploring the Meaning

5) How did the prophecy in Isaiah 52–53 portray God's Servant (the Messiah) who would come?

_____

_____

_____

6) In what ways does the prophecy in Isaiah 52–53 compare or contrast with Mark's introduction of Jesus?

_____

_____

_____

_____

7) Looking back through Mark 1–2, what happened to Christ's message when word of His miraculous power began to spread?

_____

_____

_____

8) Review Mark 1:16–29 and read Matthew 10:1–4. Jesus hand-picked His disciples to become fishers of men. For example, Simon the Zealot was so-called because he wanted to see the overthrow of Roman authority; meanwhile, Matthew the tax collector had been in cahoots with the Romans. Why do you think Jesus selected such a diverse group? What might the diversity of these men mean for the spread of the good news?

_____

_____

_____

Truth for Today

Evangelism is the purest, truest, noblest, and most essential work the church will ever do. The work of fishing men and women out of the sea of sin, the work of rescuing people from the breakers of hell, is the greatest work the church is called by God to do. Rescuing men from sin is God's great concern. Evangelism has been called the job of God. God sent His Son to earth—to preach, die, and be raised—for the very purpose of saving men from sin.

Reflecting on the Text

9) John Knox once pleaded with God, "Give me Scotland or I die." How does such a passion for telling people about Jesus compare with the programs of many modern-day churches?

_____

_____

_____

_____

10) Jesus came to bring salvation to a lost world. He gathered followers who would emulate Him in this task. What does it mean to you to be a "fisher of men"?

_____

_____

_____

11) The power and authority of Jesus are made clear in the opening chapters of Mark. In what areas of your life do you need the powerful and compassionate touch of Christ today?

_____

_____

_____

PERSONAL RESPONSE

Write out additional reflections, questions you may have, or a prayer.

_____

_____

_____

_____

_____

_____

_____

_____

_____

_____

_____

_____

2

A MIXED RESPONSE
Mark 3:1–35

DRAWING NEAR

Jesus once asked His followers, "Who do men say that I am?" (Mark 8:27). The first-century responses varied widely. Then Jesus asked His followers, "Who do you say that I am?" How would you answer that question?

_____

_____

_____

Ask God to reveal more and more to you who Jesus is as you study the book of Mark.

THE CONTEXT

After a whirlwind introduction to John the Baptist and to the inaugural events of Christ's public ministry, Mark continues his concise portrait of Jesus the Servant by comparing and contrasting the reception of Christ by the true disciples with the growing opposition to Him by the Jewish religious leaders.

Mark 3 contains the last of the "conflict" episodes (2:1–11; 13–17; 18–22; 23–28), and, as such, it provides a sense of climax to the growing antagonism between Jesus and the Jewish leaders. Like a first-rate novelist or journalist, Mark introduces this increasing tension into his plot, foreshadowing a deathly showdown to come. Specifically, it is the healing of a man's withered hand on the Sabbath that prompts the Pharisees to begin counseling together how to destroy Jesus. This, in turn, leads to Christ's withdrawal to the Sea of Galilee with a great multitude from many places, where He names the twelve apostles.

Because even Christ's own family and friends misunderstand His message and ministry, it is not surprising when Mark records blasphemous accusations by the scribes and Pharisees. This backlash results in Jesus' redefinition of what it means to relate rightly to God: all those who hear and embrace Christ's message by faith are part of God's family.

KEYS TO THE TEXT

Jewish Religious Leaders: The *Pharisees* were a small (about 6,000) legalistic sect of the Jews, who were known for their rigid adherence to the ceremonial fine points of the law. Their name means "separated ones." Jesus rebuked them for rank hypocrisy and for using human tradition to nullify Scripture. The *Sadducees* denied the resurrection of the dead and the existence of angels, and accepted only the Pentateuch as authoritative. They tended to be wealthy, aristocratic members of the priestly tribe, and in the days of Herod their sect controlled the temple. The *Herodians* were a political party of Jews who backed Herod Antipas, a puppet of Rome.

Healing on the Sabbath: The Sabbath was the day of worship and rest God ordained for His people. Jewish *tradition* prohibited the practice of medicine on the Sabbath, except in life-threatening situations. But no actual law in the Old Testament forbade the giving of medicine, healing, or any other acts of mercy on the Sabbath. Christ has the prerogative to rule over not only their man-made sabbatarian rules but also over the Sabbath itself, which was designed for worshiping God. Again, this was an inescapable claim of deity, and as such it prompted the Pharisees' violent outrage.

UNLEASHING THE TEXT

Read 3:1–35, noting the key words and definitions next to the passage.

withered hand (v. 1)—a condition of paralysis or deformity from an accident, a disease, or a congenital defect

accuse (v. 2)—The Pharisees had no desire to learn from Jesus but only a hatred for Him and a passion to destroy Him.

anger (v. 5)—holy indignation with sinful attitudes and practices

hardness of their hearts (v. 5)—the inability to understand truth because of a rebellious attitude

Mark 3:1–35 (NKJV)

1 *And He entered the synagogue again, and a man was there who had a withered hand.*

2 *So they watched Him closely, whether He would heal him on the Sabbath, so that they might accuse Him.*

3 *And He said to the man who had the withered hand, "Step forward."*

4 *Then He said to them, "Is it lawful on the Sabbath to do good or to do evil, to save life or to kill?" But they kept silent.*

5 *And when He had looked around at them with anger, being grieved by the hardness of their hearts, He said to the man, "Stretch out your hand." And he stretched it out, and his hand was restored as whole as the other.*

6 *Then the Pharisees went out and immediately plotted with the Herodians against Him, how they might destroy Him.*

7 *But Jesus withdrew with His disciples to the sea. And a great multitude from Galilee followed Him, and from Judea*

8 *and Jerusalem and Idumea and beyond the Jordan; and those from Tyre and Sidon, a great multitude, when they heard how many things He was doing, came to Him.*

9 *So He told His disciples that a small boat should be kept ready for Him because of the multitude, lest they should crush Him.*

10 *For He healed many, so that as many as had afflictions pressed about Him to touch Him.*

11 *And the unclean spirits, whenever they saw Him, fell down before Him and cried out, saying, "You are the Son of God."*

12 *But He sternly warned them that they should not make Him known.*

13 *And He went up on the mountain and called to Him those He Himself wanted. And they came to Him.*

14 *Then He appointed twelve, that they might be with Him and that He might send them out to preach,*

15 *and to have power to heal sicknesses and to cast out demons:*

16 *Simon, to whom He gave the name Peter;*

17 *James the son of Zebedee and John the brother of James, to whom He gave the name Boanerges, that is, "Sons of Thunder";*

18 *Andrew, Philip, Bartholomew, Matthew, Thomas, James the son of Alphaeus, Thaddaeus, Simon the Cananite;*

19 *and Judas Iscariot, who also betrayed Him. And they went into a house.*

20 *Then the multitude came together again, so that they could not so much as eat bread.*

21 *But when His own people heard about this, they went out to lay hold of Him, for they said, "He is out of His mind."*

22 *And the scribes who came down from Jerusalem said, "He has Beelzebub," and, "By the ruler of the demons He casts out demons."*

afflictions (v. 10)—literally, "a whip, a lash," sometimes translated "plagues," or "scourges"; a metaphorical description of agonizing physical ailments and illnesses.

unclean spirits (v. 11)— demons

appointed twelve (v. 14)—This distinct new group would constitute the foundation of the church.

Sons of Thunder (v. 17)—a probable reference to their intense, outspoken personalities

Thaddeus (v. 18)—called "Lebbaeus" in Matthew 10:3; "Judas, the son of James" in Luke and Acts; and "Judas (not Iscariot)" in John 14:22

His own people (v. 21)—in the strictest sense, "family"

scribes (v. 22)—Jewish legal scholars, also called lawyers; trained in the Mosaic law and its application

has an end (v. 26)—a reference to the ultimate doom of Satan

Assuredly, I say to you (v. 28)—a common expression introducing truthful and authoritative words from Jesus

he who blasphemes . . . never has forgiveness (v. 29)—the deliberate, disrespectful slander of the person and ministry of the Holy Spirit in pointing to the Lordship and redemption of Jesus Christ; that is, the full and complete rejection of the only basis of God's salvation

23 So He called them to Himself and said to them in parables: "How can Satan cast out Satan?

24 If a kingdom is divided against itself, that kingdom cannot stand.

25 And if a house is divided against itself, that house cannot stand.

26 And if Satan has risen up against himself, and is divided, he cannot stand, but has an end.

27 No one can enter a strong man's house and plunder his goods, unless he first binds the strong man. And then he will plunder his house.

28 "Assuredly, I say to you, all sins will be forgiven the sons of men, and whatever blasphemies they may utter;

29 but he who blasphemes against the Holy Spirit never has forgiveness, but is subject to eternal condemnation"—

30 because they said, "He has an unclean spirit."

31 Then His brothers and His mother came, and standing outside they sent to Him, calling Him.

32 And a multitude was sitting around Him; and they said to Him, "Look, Your mother and Your brothers are outside seeking You."

33 But He answered them, saying, "Who is My mother, or My brothers?"

34 And He looked around in a circle at those who sat about Him, and said, "Here are My mother and My brothers!

35 For whoever does the will of God is My brother and My sister and mother."

1) As the plot thickens, Mark identifies the main characters. List the individuals and groups that are recorded here.

_____

_____

_____

_____

2) With which group do you most identify? Why?

_____

_____

_____

3) Why was Jesus so angry with the Jewish leaders?

_____

_____

_____

(Verses to consider: Mark 11:15–18; Matt. 21:12–13; Luke 19:45–48)

4) What was the job description of the twelve men chosen by Christ to be apostles?

_____

_____

_____

5) How did Jesus' own family members respond to His ministry? Why?

_____

_____

_____

GOING DEEPER

Jesus sometimes walked away from conflict, but not this time. He had to challenge the accusation that He was one with Satan. Read the parallel passage found in Luke 11:15–23, and answer the questions below.

EXPLORING THE MEANING

6) Using Luke as our source, what do these words of Christ tell us about His power over the realm of Satan?

_____

_____

_____

7) Read 2 Corinthians 10:3–6. How do Paul's remarks about spiritual warfare underscore what Jesus is saying in Luke 11?

_____

_____

_____

8) What do you think Jesus meant when He declared that His true mother and brothers and sisters are those who do His will?

_____

_____

_____

Truth for Today

The Lord's purpose in referring to His disciples as His mother and brothers was to teach that He invites the entire world into His intimate and divine family. Anyone can enter His spiritual family by trusting in Him, and the family of God is the only family that ultimately matters.

Reflecting on the Text

9) If you had lived during the time of Christ, and had been among the masses watching and listening to Him, do you think you would have followed Him? Why or why not? What would have been some obstacles for you to follow Jesus? What would have been some incentives?

_____

_____

_____

10) What religious leaders or people today have you heard of who oppose the person and work of Christ, overtly or inadvertently? How can you avoid doing that?

_____

_____

_____

11) Jesus praises those who do His will. In what one or two specific areas do you need to conform your life more closely to the will of God?

_____

_____

_____

PERSONAL RESPONSE

Write out additional reflections, questions you may have, or a prayer.

_____

_____

_____

_____

_____

_____

_____

_____

_____

_____

_____

_____

_____

_____

_____

_____

_____

_____

_____

ADDITIONAL NOTES

3

THE SERVANT SPEAKS IN PARABLES
Mark 4:1–34

DRAWING NEAR

Jesus was a master teacher and He loved to tell stories. Who is the best teacher you have had, and why?

_____

_____

_____

What other individuals have marked your life by their ability to explain God's truth to you in a way that you could understand it?

_____

_____

_____

THE CONTEXT

Mark depicts Jesus as the ultimate Servant and as a man of action. Though Mark's emphasis is more on what Jesus did than what He said, Mark does include in his narrative some examples of the Lord's teaching.

Such is the case in Mark 4. Here we find a series of parables. The parable was a common form of Jewish teaching, and the term is found some forty-five times in the Septuagint, the Greek Old Testament. The term is a compound word made up from the Greek verb that means "to throw, lay, or place," and the prefix meaning "alongside of." Thus, the idea is that of placing or laying something alongside something else for the purpose of comparison. A spiritual truth would often be expressed by laying it alongside, so to speak, a physical example that could be more easily understood. A common, observable object or practice was used to illustrate a subjective truth or principle. The known elucidated the unknown.

Cases in point are the parables of the sower (4:1–9), the lamp (4:21–25), the seed (4:26–29), and the mustard seed (4:30–34). Mark records Jesus' explanation of the parable of the sower (4:13–20). Also, Mark gives insight into the reason Jesus employed this often misunderstood literary/oratorical device: to reveal previously unknown mysteries to believers and to conceal truth from unbelievers.

KEYS TO THE TEXT

Kingdom of God: Jesus made it clear at the beginning of His ministry that He was bringing in an altogether different kind of kingdom, which was manifest through the rule of God in people's hearts through faith in the Savior (see Luke 17:20–21). This kingdom was neither confined to a particular geographical location nor visible to human eyes. It would come quietly, invisibly, and without the normal pomp and splendor associated with the arrival of a king. This kingdom was about serving, not power.

UNLEASHING THE TEXT

Read 4:1–34, noting the key words and definitions next to the passage.

Mark 4:1–34 (NKJV)

1 And again He began to teach by the sea. And a great multitude was gathered to Him, so that He got into a boat and sat in it on the sea; and the whole multitude was on the land facing the sea.

2 Then He taught them many things by parables, and said to them in His teaching:

3 "Listen! Behold, a sower went out to sow.

wayside (v. 4)—either a road near the field's edge or a path that traversed a field, both of which were hard surfaces from constant foot traffic

4 And it happened, as he sowed, that some seed fell by the wayside; and the birds of the air came and devoured it.

stony ground (v. 5)—beds of rock just under the topsoil that prevent plants from developing a hardy root system

5 Some fell on stony ground, where it did not have much earth; and immediately it sprang up because it had no depth of earth.

6 But when the sun was up it was scorched, and because it had no root it withered away.

7 And some seed fell among thorns; and the thorns grew up and choked it, and it yielded no crop.

increased . . . a hundred (v. 8)— The average ratio of harvested grain to sown seed was 8 to 1, or sometimes a very exceptional 10 to 1.

8 But other seed fell on good ground and yielded a crop that sprang up, increased and produced: some thirtyfold, some sixty, and some a hundred."

"He who has ears to hear" (v. 9)—Jesus' thinly veiled announcement that spiritual discernment and divine insight are necessary for apprehending God's truth

9 And He said to them, "He who has ears to hear, let him hear!"

10 But when He was alone, those around Him with the twelve asked Him about the parable.

11 And He said to them, "To you it has been given to know the mystery of the kingdom of God; but to

those who are outside, all things come in parables,

12 so that 'Seeing they may see and not perceive, And hearing they may hear and not understand; Lest they should turn, And their sins be forgiven them.'"

13 And He said to them, "Do you not understand this parable? How then will you understand all the parables?

14 The sower sows the word.

15 And these are the ones by the wayside where the word is sown. When they hear, Satan comes immediately and takes away the word that was sown in their hearts.

16 These likewise are the ones sown on stony ground who, when they hear the word, immediately receive it with gladness;

17 and they have no root in themselves, and so endure only for a time. Afterward, when tribulation or persecution arises for the word's sake, immediately they stumble.

18 Now these are the ones sown among thorns; they are the ones who hear the word,

19 and the cares of this world, the deceitfulness of riches, and the desires for other things entering in choke the word, and it becomes unfruitful.

20 But these are the ones sown on good ground, those who hear the word, accept it, and bear fruit: some thirtyfold, some sixty, and some a hundred."

21 Also He said to them, "Is a lamp brought to be put under a basket or under a bed? Is it not to be set on a lampstand?

22 For there is nothing hidden which will not be revealed, nor has anything been kept secret but that it should come to light.

23 If anyone has ears to hear, let him hear."

24 Then He said to them, "Take heed what you hear. With the same measure you use, it will be measured to you; and to you who hear, more will be given.

25 For whoever has, to him more will be given; but whoever does not have, even what he has will be taken away from him."

mystery (v. 11)— something previously hidden in the Old Testament and made known in the New Testament; in this case, the kingdom of heaven

those who are outside (v. 11)— unbelievers, non-followers of Christ

the word (v. 14)—the gospel of salvation

tribulation or persecution (v. 17)—not routine difficulties and troubles, but the suffering and trials that come due to one's association with Christ

stumble (v. 17)—literally, "to fall" or "to cause offense"; from which we get our English term "scandalize"

cares of this world (v. 19)— literally, "the distractions of this age"

with the same measure (v. 24)—that is, the law of sowing and reaping; rewards or results are tied to the effort put forth

26 *And He said, "The kingdom of God is as if a man should scatter seed on the ground,*

27 *and should sleep by night and rise by day, and the seed should sprout and grow, he himself does not know how.*

28 *For the earth yields crops by itself: first the blade, then the head, after that the full grain in the head.*

29 *But when the grain ripens, immediately he puts in the sickle, because the harvest has come."*

30 *Then He said, "To what shall we liken the kingdom of God? Or with what parable shall we picture it?*

31 *It is like a mustard seed which, when it is sown on the ground, is smaller than all the seeds on earth;*

32 *but when it is sown, it grows up and becomes greater than all herbs, and shoots out large branches, so that the birds of the air may nest under its shade."*

33 *And with many such parables He spoke the word to them as they were able to hear it.*

34 *But without a parable He did not speak to them. And when they were alone, He explained all things to His disciples.*

a mustard seed (v. 31)—the seed of the common black mustard plant, used as a condiment and also for medicinal purposes

smaller than all (v. 31)—smaller than all the other seeds sown by Jews in Palestine

1) According to this parable, what different responses are possible when God's word is proclaimed?

_____

_____

2) What reason did Jesus give for teaching in parables? What does this mean?

_____

_____

3) What comment of Jesus from the "parable of the lamp" reveals that Jesus intended for the whole world to hear the gospel?

_____

_____

_____

GOING DEEPER

As a cross-reference comparison, read the version of the parable of the sower in Matthew 13:1–23.

EXPLORING THE MEANING

4) What additional insights do you glean when you lay Matthew's account next to Mark's version?

_____

_____

_____

5) What is (are) the implication(s) of the parable of the mustard seed?

_____

_____

_____

6) Read 1 Corinthians 2:13–16. How do Paul's comments here underscore the points that Jesus makes in Mark 4?

_____

_____

_____

TRUTH FOR TODAY

To those who are considering His claims or have made a perfunctory decision for Him, Jesus gives an appeal to think about the kind of soil that represents their heart. If it is hard-packed and beaten down by continual neglect of God, or perhaps even by conscious opposition, He calls that person to allow His Spirit to break up the ground and make it receptive to His Word. If the soil of a person's heart is shallow and superficial, He calls that person to allow the Spirit to remove the rocky resistance that lies beneath the surface of his seeming acceptance of the gospel and give him true faith. If the soil of a person's heart is infested with the weedy cares and concerns of the world, He asks that person to allow the Spirit to cleanse him of his worldliness and to receive Him with no reservations or competing loyalties.

REFLECTING ON THE TEXT

7) Rather than lecturing His audiences with obscure theological words and ideas, Jesus, the master teacher, told down-to-earth stories about everyday life. He related simple parables to His listeners, featuring common objects and practices. Why are stories like this so effective in communicating spiritual truth?

_____

_____

_____

8) What kind of soil described by Jesus best matches your own spiritual condition just now? Why? What needs to change?

_____

_____

_____

9) List below the people who teach or minister to you in some way (your pastor, Sunday school teacher, small group leader, radio preacher, and so forth). Pray for them this week, that they would communicate God's truth faithfully, clearly, and effectively.

_____

_____

PERSONAL RESPONSE

Write out additional reflections, questions you may have, or a prayer.

_____

_____

_____

_____

_____

_____

4

THE SERVANT DEMONSTRATES HIS POWER
Mark 4:35–5:43

DRAWING NEAR

Put a check mark by the following hardships you have experienced. Draw a circle around the ones you fear the most.

_____ sickness	_____ physical pain	_____ emotional pain
_____ economic hardship	_____ poverty	_____ war
_____ disease	_____ natural disaster	_____ injustice
_____ political persecution	_____ hunger	_____ grief
_____ crime	_____ accidents	_____ injury
_____ long-term health problems	_____ demonic attack	_____ death

In what ways does knowing that Jesus is Lord of everything help to alleviate your fears?

_____

_____

_____

THE CONTEXT

The key verse in Mark is, "For even the Son of Man did not come to be served, but to serve, and to give His life a ransom for many" (10:45). One way Jesus served those He came to save was by delivering God's truth to a world shrouded in darkness. Another way He served was by miraculously delivering people from certain temporal trials. These assorted miracles were not ends in themselves, but rather a means to a greater end. They were signs, intended to point out deeper truths about the person and work of Christ. They acted to authenticate His message.

Above all else the miracles were foretastes of kingdom power. When Jesus healed diseases and restored broken bodies, He provided a glimpse into the kingdom where there would be no sickness or deformity. When He cast out demons, He gave a preview of the kingdom where there would be no demonic activity. When He raised the dead, He previewed the kingdom where there would be no death.

In this next portion, Mark adds to an already convincing presentation of Jesus as the Servant sent by God by showing Christ's awesome power over the natural realm, over the supernatural realm, over sickness, and even over death.

KEYS TO THE TEXT

Miracles: In all of Old Testament history there was never a time or a person who exhibited such extensive healing power as Jesus. Physical healings were very rare in the Old Testament. Christ chose to display His deity by healing, raising the dead, and liberating people from demons. That not only showed the Messiah's power over the physical and spiritual realms, but also demonstrated the compassion of God toward those affected by sin.

Unclean Spirits, Demons: The term "unclean spirit" is used interchangeably in the New Testament with "demon." When Lucifer (Satan) fell, he took a third of the angels with him (see Rev. 12:3–4). These fallen angels are nothing but demonic beings, some of whom are still troubling the earth to this very day—and will continue to do so until they are destroyed by the hand of God's judgment. Satan and his demon hosts opposed Jesus' work throughout His ministry. Jesus always triumphed over their futile efforts (see Col. 2:15), convincingly demonstrating His ultimate victory by His resurrection. There were many times when demons looked at Jesus and contemplated the truth of His character and identity. "You are the Son of God" (1:24). The demons unhesitatingly affirmed the uniqueness of Jesus' nature, which Mark saw as clear proof of Jesus' deity. (*The Glory of Heaven: The Truth about Heaven, Angels, and Eternal Life*)

UNLEASHING THE TEXT

Read 4:35–5:43, noting the key words and definitions next to the passage.

Mark 4:35–5:43 (NKJV)

35 *On the same day, when evening had come, He said to them, "Let us cross over to the other side."*

36 *Now when they had left the multitude, they took Him along in the boat as He was. And other little boats were also with Him.*

great windstorm (4:37)—The Greek word can mean "whirlwind," a severe and sudden storm.

37 *And a great windstorm arose, and the waves beat into the boat, so that it was already filling.*

38 *But He was in the stern, asleep on a pillow. And they awoke Him and said to Him, "Teacher, do*

You not care that we are perishing?"

39 Then He arose and rebuked the wind, and said to the sea, "Peace, be still!" And the wind ceased and there was a great calm.

40 But He said to them, "Why are you so fearful? How is it that you have no faith?"

41 And they feared exceedingly, and said to one another, "Who can this be, that even the wind and the sea obey Him!"

5:1 Then they came to the other side of the sea, to the country of the Gadarenes.

2 And when He had come out of the boat, immediately there met Him out of the tombs a man with an unclean spirit,

3 who had his dwelling among the tombs; and no one could bind him, not even with chains,

4 because he had often been bound with shackles and chains. And the chains had been pulled apart by him, and the shackles broken in pieces; neither could anyone tame him.

5 And always, night and day, he was in the mountains and in the tombs, crying out and cutting himself with stones.

6 When he saw Jesus from afar, he ran and worshiped Him.

7 And he cried out with a loud voice and said, "What have I to do with You, Jesus, Son of the Most High God? I implore You by God that You do not torment me."

8 For He said to him, "Come out of the man, unclean spirit!"

9 Then He asked him, "What is your name?" And he answered, saying, "My name is Legion; for we are many."

10 Also he begged Him earnestly that He would not send them out of the country.

11 Now a large herd of swine was feeding there near the mountains.

12 So all the demons begged Him, saying, "Send us to the swine, that we may enter them."

"Peace, be still!" (v. 39)—literally, "be silent, be muzzled"; a command for the storm to cease completely and immediately, not a gradual subsiding

the tombs (5:2)—Cemeteries were common dwelling places for the demented of that day.

unclean spirit (v. 2)—the morally filthy demons who controlled the man, causing him so much harm

Most High God (v. 7)—an ancient title used by both Jews and Gentiles to identify the one, true, and living God of Israel and distinguish Him from all false idol gods

Legion (v. 9)—a Latin term that defined a Roman military unit of 6,000 soldiers; the man was controlled by a large number of militant evil spirits *sitting . . . in his right mind* (v. 15)—a major contrast with his former agitated, restless, self-destructive state

13 *And at once Jesus gave them permission. Then the unclean spirits went out and entered the swine (there were about two thousand); and the herd ran violently down the steep place into the sea, and drowned in the sea.*

14 *So those who fed the swine fled, and they told it in the city and in the country. And they went out to see what it was that had happened.*

15 *Then they came to Jesus, and saw the one who had been demon-possessed and had the legion, sitting and clothed and in his right mind. And they were afraid.*

16 *And those who saw it told them how it happened to him who had been demon-possessed, and about the swine.*

plead with Him to depart from their region (v. 17)—probably out of concern of more economic loss; certainly out of spiritual blindness and hard-heartedness

17 *Then they began to plead with Him to depart from their region.*

18 *And when He got into the boat, he who had been demon-possessed begged Him that he might be with Him.*

19 *However, Jesus did not permit him, but said to him, "Go home to your friends, and tell them what great things the Lord has done for you, and how He has had compassion on you."*

Decapolis (v. 20)—a league of ten Greek-influenced cities east of the Jordan River

20 *And he departed and began to proclaim in Decapolis all that Jesus had done for him; and all marveled.*

21 *Now when Jesus had crossed over again by boat to the other side, a great multitude gathered to Him; and He was by the sea.*

22 *And behold, one of the rulers of the synagogue came, Jairus by name. And when he saw Him, he fell at His feet*

23 *and begged Him earnestly, saying, "My little daughter lies at the point of death. Come and lay Your hands on her, that she may be healed, and she will live."*

24 *So Jesus went with him, and a great multitude followed Him and thronged Him.*

25 *Now a certain woman had a flow of blood for twelve years,*

26 *and had suffered many things from many physicians. She had spent all that she had and was no better, but rather grew worse.*

27 *When she heard about Jesus, she came behind Him in the crowd and touched His garment.*

28 *For she said, "If only I may touch His clothes, I shall be made well."*

29 *Immediately the fountain of her blood was dried up, and she felt in her body that she was healed of the affliction.*

30 *And Jesus, immediately knowing in Himself that power had gone out of Him, turned around in the crowd and said, "Who touched My clothes?"*

31 *But His disciples said to Him, "You see the multitude thronging You, and You say, 'Who touched Me?'"*

32 *And He looked around to see her who had done this thing.*

33 *But the woman, fearing and trembling, knowing what had happened to her, came and fell down before Him and told Him the whole truth.*

34 *And He said to her, "Daughter, your faith has made you well. Go in peace, and be healed of your affliction."*

35 *While He was still speaking, some came from the ruler of the synagogue's house who said, "Your daughter is dead. Why trouble the Teacher any further?"*

36 *As soon as Jesus heard the word that was spoken, He said to the ruler of the synagogue, "Do not be afraid; only believe."*

37 *And He permitted no one to follow Him except Peter, James, and John the brother of James.*

38 *Then He came to the house of the ruler of the synagogue, and saw a tumult and those who wept and wailed loudly.*

39 *When He came in, He said to them, "Why make this commotion and weep? The child is not dead, but sleeping."*

flow of blood (v. 25)—a chronic internal hemorrhage, perhaps from a tumor or other disease

fountain of her blood (v. 29)—the source of the bleeding

"Who touched my clothes?" (v. 30)—a question asked, not out of ignorance, but to draw the woman out of the crowd and allow her to praise God for what had happened

Peter, James, and John (v. 37)—Christ's "inner circle" of disciples, who were frequently allowed to witness events from which the other disciples were excluded

those who wept and wailed loudly (v. 38)—probably paid mourners; it was customary to pay people to mourn at funerals *ridiculed* (v. 40)— literally, "laughed Him to scorn" or "were laughing in His face"; an irreverent, foolish reaction highlighting their naturalistic thinking and intended to humiliate the Lord

"Talitha, cumi" (v. 41)—Jesus spoke Aramaic.

40 *And they ridiculed Him. But when He had put them all outside, He took the father and the mother of the child, and those who were with Him, and entered where the child was lying.*

41 *Then He took the child by the hand, and said to her, "Talitha, cumi," which is translated, "Little girl, I say to you, arise."*

42 *Immediately the girl arose and walked, for she was twelve years of age. And they were overcome with great amazement.*

43 *But He commanded them strictly that no one should know it, and said that something should be given her to eat.*

1) How did the disciples respond to the storm? To Jesus' calming of the storm?

_____

_____

_____

_____

(Verses to consider: Luke 5:8; John 20:26–28)

2) What does Mark's record say about the power and number of the demons who controlled the Gadarene man? What was their effect on him?

_____

_____

_____

_____

3) Who was Jairus, and why is it significant that he came to Christ for help? What "tests of faith" did he have to endure before his daughter was restored to him?

_____

_____

_____

Going Deeper

The Bible is its own best commentary, and the Old Testament often sheds light on the New Testament. Read Jeremiah's prayer and God's answer in Jeremiah 32:17–27.

Exploring the Meaning

4) How does Jeremiah 32:17–27 show God's limitless power and underscore the truth of Mark 4:35–5:43?

_____

_____

_____

5) The disciples seemed shocked and surprised by Christ's power; however, the synagogue official and the bleeding woman seemed to have great faith in the power of Christ. How do you explain the difference in their responses?

_____

_____

_____

_____

6) With which person or group of people from this extended passage do you identify most (the disciples in the storm, the man oppressed by demons, the prominent man with the sick child, or the woman with a debilitating and shameful illness)? Why?

_____

_____

_____

Truth for Today

In Christ there is no longer reason to fear sickness, disease, demons, deformity, tragedy, or even death. As believers, we can even rejoice in dying because our Lord has conquered death. Though we will not be brought back to this life, we will be raised to new life. In Him is fullness of joy and life everlasting. "No longer must the mourners weep," a poet reminds us, "nor call departed children dead, for death is transformed into sleep and every grave becomes a bed."

Reflecting on the Text

The Canadian scientist G. B. Hardy once said, "When I look at religion, I have two questions. One: Has anybody ever conquered death? and two: If they have, did they make a way for me to conquer death? I checked the tomb of Buddha, and it was occupied. I checked the tomb of Confucius and it was occupied. I came to the tomb of Jesus and it was empty. And I said, 'There is one who conquered death.' And I asked the second question, 'Did He make a way for me to do it?' I opened the Bible and discovered that He said, 'Because I live ye shall live also.' "

7) What are the implications for your life that Jesus has power and authority over all things—even death?

_____

_____

8) The common response to the power of Jesus was that people stood in awe, wonder, and amazement. When was the last time that you marveled at the power of Christ over all things?

_____

_____

9) In what area of your life do you need Christ's powerful touch today? Write a prayer of praise below and conclude it by trusting God to do the impossible in your situation.

_____

_____

Personal Response

Write out additional reflections, questions you may have, or a prayer.

_____

_____

_____

_____

5

THE SERVANT PREPARES THE TWELVE
Mark 6:1–56

DRAWING NEAR

How do you respond when you hear the word "ministry"?

_____

_____

_____

Do you think every Christian can or should have a ministry? Why or why not?

_____

_____

_____

THE CONTEXT

Until this stage of His ministry, Jesus had ministered alone. He had the companionship of the twelve disciples and the company of vast multitudes who followed wherever He went. But none of the Twelve nor the multitudes participated in His ministry except as observers or recipients. With hostility among the Jewish leaders growing, Jesus began the preliminary stages of commissioning the Twelve to join Him as fellow workers. For the balance of His earthly ministry, these men would become the primary object of Jesus' concern, instruction, and training because the establishing of His Church would soon fall squarely upon their shoulders.

Chapter 6 describes Jesus' final visit to unbelieving Nazareth, the commissioning of the Twelve, the first ministry/mission of the disciples, the violent opposition of Herod Antipas to John the Baptist and his message of repentance, the return of the twelve and their withdrawal with Jesus to Galilee, the miraculous feeding of the 5,000 and the aftermath of that incident, Jesus walking on the water during a storm at sea, and some healing ministry at Gennesaret.

KEYS TO THE TEXT

Ministry: A distinctive biblical idea that means "to serve" or "service." In the Old Testament the word "servant" was used primarily for court servants (1 Kings

10:5; Esther 1:10). During the period between the Old and New Testaments, it came to be used in connection with ministering to the poor. This use of the word is close to the work of the seven in waiting on tables in the New Testament (Acts 6:1–7). In reality, all believers are "ministers." The apostle Paul urged the true pastor-teacher to "equip the saints" so they can minister to one another (Eph. 4:11–12). The model, of course, is Jesus, who "did not come to be served, but to serve" (Mark 10:45). Jesus equated service to God with service to others. When we minister to the needs of the hungry or the lonely, we actually minister to Christ (Matt. 25:31–46). And when we fail to do so, we sin against God (James 2:14–17; 4:17). In this light, all who took part in the fellowship of service were ministers. (*Nelson's New Illustrated Bible Dictionary*)

UNLEASHING THE TEXT

Read 6:1–56, noting the key words and definitions next to the passage.

Mark 6:1–56 (NKJV)

His own country (v. 1)—Nazareth, Jesus' hometown

astonished (v. 2)—marked by skepticism and a critical attitude

carpenter (v. 3)—Jesus had obvious training and experience in Joseph's trade.

offended (v. 3)—literally, "scandalize, to stumble or become ensnared"; that is, they refused to accept His credentials

two by two (v. 7)—a wise practice ensuring help, encouragement, and the validity of their witness

1 Then He went out from there and came to His own country, and His disciples followed Him.

2 And when the Sabbath had come, He began to teach in the synagogue. And many hearing Him were astonished, saying, "Where did this Man get these things? And what wisdom is this which is given to Him, that such mighty works are performed by His hands!

3 Is this not the carpenter, the Son of Mary, and brother of James, Joses, Judas, and Simon? And are not His sisters here with us?" So they were offended at Him.

4 But Jesus said to them, "A prophet is not without honor except in his own country, among his own relatives, and in his own house."

5 Now He could do no mighty work there, except that He laid His hands on a few sick people and healed them.

6 And He marveled because of their unbelief. Then He went about the villages in a circuit, teaching.

7 And He called the twelve to Himself, and began to send them out two by two, and gave them power over unclean spirits.

8 *He commanded them to take nothing for the journey except a staff—no bag, no bread, no copper in their money belts—*

9 *but to wear sandals, and not to put on two tunics.*

10 *Also He said to them, "In whatever place you enter a house, stay there till you depart from that place.*

11 *And whoever will not receive you nor hear you, when you depart from there, shake off the dust under your feet as a testimony against them. Assuredly, I say to you, it will be more tolerable for Sodom and Gomorrah in the day of judgment than for that city!"*

12 *So they went out and preached that people should repent.*

13 *And they cast out many demons, and anointed with oil many who were sick, and healed them.*

14 *Now King Herod heard of Him, for His name had become well known. And he said, "John the Baptist is risen from the dead, and therefore these powers are at work in him."*

15 *Others said, "It is Elijah." And others said, "It is the Prophet, or like one of the prophets."*

16 *But when Herod heard, he said, "This is John, whom I beheaded; he has been raised from the dead!"*

17 *For Herod himself had sent and laid hold of John, and bound him in prison for the sake of Herodias, his brother Philip's wife; for he had married her.*

18 *Because John had said to Herod, "It is not lawful for you to have your brother's wife."*

19 *Therefore Herodias held it against him and wanted to kill him, but she could not;*

20 *for Herod feared John, knowing that he was a just and holy man, and he protected him. And when he heard him, he did many things, and heard him gladly.*

21 *Then an opportune day came when Herod on his birthday gave a feast for his nobles, the high officers, and the chief men of Galilee.*

22 *And when Herodias' daughter herself came in and*

---

not to put on two tunics (v. 9)— Wearing two would symbolize wealth; one would help them identify with common people.

shake off the dust (v. 11)—a symbolic act of renouncing fellowship with those who rejected the gospel

anointed with oil . . . sick (v. 13)—Olive oil had medicinal use, and here it also symbolizes the presence of the Holy Spirit.

John had said . . . It is not lawful (v. 18)—The tense of the Greek verb suggests repeated confrontations of Herod by John.

he did many things (v. 20)—or "he was very perplexed," suggesting great inner turmoil in Herod as a result of John's rebukes

danced (v. 22)—suggests highly suggestive choreography, similar to a modern striptease

danced, and pleased Herod and those who sat with him, the king said to the girl, "Ask me whatever you want, and I will give it to you."

23 He also swore to her, "Whatever you ask me, I will give you, up to half my kingdom."

24 So she went out and said to her mother, "What shall I ask?" And she said, "The head of John the Baptist!"

25 Immediately she came in with haste to the king and asked, saying, "I want you to give me at once the head of John the Baptist on a platter."

26 And the king was exceedingly sorry; yet, because of the oaths and because of those who sat with him, he did not want to refuse her.

27 Immediately the king sent an executioner and commanded his head to be brought. And he went and beheaded him in prison,

28 brought his head on a platter, and gave it to the girl; and the girl gave it to her mother.

29 When his disciples heard of it, they came and took away his corpse and laid it in a tomb.

30 Then the apostles gathered to Jesus and told Him all things, both what they had done and what they had taught.

by yourselves (v. 31)—Jesus recognized the need of the twelve for some rest and privacy after their tiring ministry endeavor.

31 And He said to them, "Come aside by yourselves to a deserted place and rest a while." For there were many coming and going, and they did not even have time to eat.

32 So they departed to a deserted place in the boat by themselves.

33 But the multitudes saw them departing, and many knew Him and ran there on foot from all the cities. They arrived before them and came together to Him.

was moved with compassion (v. 34)—from the Greek word referring to the intestines or bowels, thus a deep, internal caring comparable to the modern expressions of deep feeling such as "broken-hearted" or "gut-wrenching"

34 And Jesus, when He came out, saw a great multitude and was moved with compassion for them, because they were like sheep not having a shepherd. So He began to teach them many things.

35 When the day was now far spent, His disciples came to Him and said, "This is a deserted place, and already the hour is late.

36 *Send them away, that they may go into the surrounding country and villages and buy themselves bread; for they have nothing to eat."*

37 *But He answered and said to them, "You give them something to eat." And they said to Him, "Shall we go and buy two hundred denarii worth of bread and give them something to eat?"*

38 *But He said to them, "How many loaves do you have? Go and see." And when they found out they said, "Five, and two fish."*

39 *Then He commanded them to make them all sit down in groups on the green grass.*

40 *So they sat down in ranks, in hundreds and in fifties.*

41 *And when He had taken the five loaves and the two fish, He looked up to heaven, blessed and broke the loaves, and gave them to His disciples to set before them; and the two fish He divided among them all.*

42 *So they all ate and were filled.*

43 *And they took up twelve baskets full of fragments and of the fish.*

44 *Now those who had eaten the loaves were about five thousand men.*

45 *Immediately He made His disciples get into the boat and go before Him to the other side, to Bethsaida, while He sent the multitude away.*

46 *And when He had sent them away, He departed to the mountain to pray.*

47 *Now when evening came, the boat was in the middle of the sea; and He was alone on the land.*

48 *Then He saw them straining at rowing, for the wind was against them. Now about the fourth watch of the night He came to them, walking on the sea, and would have passed them by.*

49 *And when they saw Him walking on the sea, they supposed it was a ghost, and cried out;*

50 *for they all saw Him and were troubled. But immediately He talked with them and said to them, "Be of good cheer! It is I; do not be afraid."*

two hundred denarii (v. 37)— two hundred days' (or eight months') worth of pay

five thousand men (v. 44)—The word refers strictly to males, suggesting a far greater number, perhaps as many as twenty thousand, when including women and children.

fourth watch (v. 48)—3:00 AM to 6:00 AM

they had not understood about the loaves (v. 52)—The disciples had not yet grasped the supernatural identity of Jesus, otherwise they would not have been shocked to see Him walking on water.

51 Then He went up into the boat to them, and the wind ceased. And they were greatly amazed in themselves beyond measure, and marveled.

52 For they had not understood about the loaves, because their heart was hardened.

53 When they had crossed over, they came to the land of Gennesaret and anchored there.

54 And when they came out of the boat, immediately the people recognized Him,

55 ran through that whole surrounding region, and began to carry about on beds those who were sick to wherever they heard He was.

56 Wherever He entered, into villages, cities, or the country, they laid the sick in the marketplaces, and begged Him that they might just touch the hem of His garment. And as many as touched Him were made well.

1) What happened when Jesus returned to Nazareth, His hometown, and taught in the synagogue? What lessons did the disciples likely learn from this incident?

_____

_____

_____

2) Based on the instructions Jesus gave, what were some lessons He wanted His disciples to learn on their first ministry trip?

_____

_____

_____

3) What can we learn about Herod Antipas from the description found in Mark 6?

_____

_____

_____

4) What do you learn about Jesus from His response to the crowds, even when He was tired and spent (6:31–34)?

_____

_____

_____

Going Deeper

The parallel passage in Matthew 10:16–42 describes Jesus giving His disciples additional instructions prior to their first ministry trip. Read this and then answer the questions below.

Exploring the Meaning

5) It is obvious from Matthew's Gospel that Mark only recorded a small portion of Jesus' charge to His disciples. What do these additional instructions add? What is the tone of Jesus' instructions?

_____

_____

_____

6) What do you think the disciples were feeling as they heard these words? What strengths do you see in the disciples? What weaknesses?

_____

_____

_____

7) What lessons should the disciples have learned about Jesus through His feeding of the five thousand? Through His walking on water?

_____

_____

_____

_____

8) What evidence do you see in this chapter that ministering to others can be stressful?

_____

_____

_____

_____

Truth for Today

In a general sense *every* believer is commissioned by the Lord and is bound to obey His call to go and present Him to the world. Not every believer is called to be a preacher, teacher, pastor, or missionary; but every believer is called to be Christ's witness to the world. Jesus Christ has no followers who are not under His order in the Great Commission to "make disciples of all the nations" (Matthew 28:19). The first and most essential element for ministry is the unqualified understanding that one is sovereignly called, gifted, and empowered by the Lord to do His work in His way. Children of God do not determine their own destiny or mark out their own patterns or plans. They are under divine orders, and their supreme, overarching concern must be to submit to Christ in all things.

Reflecting on the Text

9) How does Jesus' style of preparing people for ministry compare with the typical approaches of training clergy and/or lay people today?

_____

_____

_____

10) After seeing Jesus and His disciples in action, how would you define "ministry" now? What kind of service for others can you get involved in?

_____

_____

_____

_____

11) How do you think someone can tell if he or she is over-involved in ministry?

_____

_____

_____

12) What one truth from this study needs special attention right now in your life? What is your plan to implement this truth into your life?

_____

_____

_____

Personal Response

Write out additional reflections, questions you may have, or a prayer.

_____

_____

_____

_____

_____

_____

_____

_____

_____

_____

_____

_____

_____

_____

ADDITIONAL NOTES

6

THE SERVANT BROADENS HIS MINISTRY
Mark 7:1–8:38

DRAWING NEAR

Religious traditions are not inherently good or bad. They can be useful in reminding us of what is true and important. But they can also be detrimental if we allow them to become larger than life and supersede God's eternal principles. Think back on your upbringing. What religious traditions were part of your family life?

_____

_____

_____

What religious traditions or rituals do you practice today? Why?

_____

_____

_____

THE CONTEXT

Ironically, the most religious people of the day had the least faith in Jesus, even as so many religious outcasts trusted and obeyed Him. After being rejected by His own people, Jesus broadened His ministry and turned His attention to the irreligious Gentiles in the area. Chapters 7 and 8 record Jesus' increasing conflict with the scribes and Pharisees over their burdensome, human-made traditions. We see Jesus' amazing healing and miracles done in Tyre, Sidon, Decapolis, and Bethsaida, as well as hear the first direct prediction of His imminent crucifixion and resurrection. This exciting passage is filled with pathos, action, and intrigue. It shows us what is required of true disciples, and reminds us that pleasing God has little to do with religious ritual and everything to do with unwavering trust in and obedience to Christ.

KEYS TO THE TEXT

Sin: Jesus said, "Evil things proceed from within and defile the man." This is the doctrine of total depravity or "original sin." This means sinners have no ability to do spiritual good or work for their own salvation from sin. They are so completely disinclined to love righteousness, so thoroughly dead in sin, that they are not able to save themselves or even to fit themselves for God's salvation. Because of Adam's sin, this state of spiritual death called total depravity has passed to all mankind (see Rom. 5:19). Sin flows from the very soul of our being. The fact that God gives "more grace" shows that His grace is greater than the power of sin, the flesh, the world, and Satan (see Rom. 5:20). Who obtains God's grace? The humble, not the proud enemies of God.

UNLEASHING THE TEXT

Read 7:1–8:38, noting the key words and definitions next to the passage.

Mark 7:1–8:38 (NKJV)

defiled (v. 2)—The disciples were being accused of being morally and spiritually polluted by eating with hands not ceremonially cleansed.

wash (v. 3)—not a cleaning of dirty hands, but a ceremonial rinsing

tradition of the elders (v. 3)— a reference to the body of extra-biblical laws and interpretations of Scripture that had actually replaced the Scriptures as the highest religious authority in Judaism

hypocrites (v. 6)—religious phonies guilty of thoughtless conformity to human laws and lacking pure hearts of genuine love and devotion for God

1 Then the Pharisees and some of the scribes came together to Him, having come from Jerusalem.

2 Now when they saw some of His disciples eat bread with defiled, that is, with unwashed hands, they found fault.

3 For the Pharisees and all the Jews do not eat unless they wash their hands in a special way, holding the tradition of the elders.

4 When they come from the marketplace, they do not eat unless they wash. And there are many other things which they have received and hold, like the washing of cups, pitchers, copper vessels, and couches.

5 Then the Pharisees and scribes asked Him, "Why do Your disciples not walk according to the tradition of the elders, but eat bread with unwashed hands?"

6 He answered and said to them, "Well did Isaiah prophesy of you hypocrites, as it is written: 'This people honors Me with their lips, But their heart is far from Me.

7 And in vain they worship Me, Teaching as doctrines the commandments of men.'

8 For laying aside the commandment of God, you hold the tradition of men— the washing of pitchers and cups, and many other such things you do."

9 He said to them, "All too well you reject the commandment of God, that you may keep your tradition.

10 For Moses said, 'Honor your father and your mother'; and, 'He who curses father or mother, let him be put to death.'

11 But you say, 'If a man says to his father or mother, "Whatever profit you might have received from me is Corban"—' (that is, a gift to God),

12 then you no longer let him do anything for his father or his mother,

13 making the word of God of no effect through your tradition which you have handed down. And many such things you do."

14 When He had called all the multitude to Himself, He said to them, "Hear Me, everyone, and understand:

15 There is nothing that enters a man from outside which can defile him; but the things which come out of him, those are the things that defile a man.

16 If anyone has ears to hear, let him hear!"

17 When He had entered a house away from the crowd, His disciples asked Him concerning the parable.

18 So He said to them, "Are you thus without understanding also? Do you not perceive that whatever enters a man from outside cannot defile him,

19 because it does not enter his heart but his stomach, and is eliminated, thus purifying all foods?"

20 And He said, "What comes out of a man, that defiles a man.

21 For from within, out of the heart of men, proceed evil thoughts, adulteries, fornications, murders,

22 thefts, covetousness, wickedness, deceit, lewdness, an evil eye, blasphemy, pride, foolishness.

23 All these evil things come from within and defile a man."

24 From there He arose and went to the region of Tyre and Sidon. And He entered a house and wanted no one to know it, but He could not be hidden.

Corban (v. 11)—a Hebrew term meaning, "given to God"; a reference to any gift or sacrifice dedicated to God and thus reserved only for sacred purposes

making the word of God of no effect (v. 13)—to deprive of authority or cancel; by elevating human traditions, the Pharisees were arrogantly denying the authority of Scripture over their lives

purifying all foods (v. 19)—By overturning the tradition of hand washing, Jesus in effect removed the restrictions regarding dietary laws.

lewdness (v. 22)—unrestrained, shameless behavior

evil eye (v. 22)—a Hebrew expression for envy or jealousy

wanted no one to know (v. 24)—Jesus did not seek a public ministry in this area, probably due to a desire to rest from the pressure of the Jewish leaders and an eagerness to further prepare His disciples.

Greek (v. 26)—a non-Jew in both language and religion

the children's bread (v. 27)—Jesus was testing the woman's faith and stating that God's blessings via the gospel were to go to the Jews first, and then to the Gentiles.

little dogs (v. 27)—pets, not the derisive, common term for mangy, vicious mongrels

25 *For a woman whose young daughter had an unclean spirit heard about Him, and she came and fell at His feet.*

26 *The woman was a Greek, a Syro-Phoenician by birth, and she kept asking Him to cast the demon out of her daughter.*

27 *But Jesus said to her, "Let the children be filled first, for it is not good to take the children's bread and throw it to the little dogs."*

28 *And she answered and said to Him, "Yes, Lord, yet even the little dogs under the table eat from the children's crumbs."*

29 *Then He said to her, "For this saying go your way; the demon has gone out of your daughter."*

30 *And when she had come to her house, she found the demon gone out, and her daughter lying on the bed.*

31 *Again, departing from the region of Tyre and Sidon, He came through the midst of the region of Decapolis to the Sea of Galilee.*

32 *Then they brought to Him one who was deaf and had an impediment in his speech, and they begged Him to put His hand on him.*

33 *And He took him aside from the multitude, and put His fingers in his ears, and He spat and touched his tongue.*

34 *Then, looking up to heaven, He sighed, and said to him, "Ephphatha," that is, "Be opened."*

35 *Immediately his ears were opened, and the impediment of his tongue was loosed, and he spoke plainly.*

36 *Then He commanded them that they should tell no one; but the more He commanded them, the more widely they proclaimed it.*

37 *And they were astonished beyond measure, saying, "He has done all things well. He makes both the deaf to hear and the mute to speak."*

8:1 *In those days, the multitude being very great and having nothing to eat, Jesus called His disciples to Him and said to them,*

2 "I have compassion on the multitude, because they have now continued with Me three days and have nothing to eat.

3 And if I send them away hungry to their own houses, they will faint on the way; for some of them have come from afar."

4 Then His disciples answered Him, "How can one satisfy these people with bread here in the wilderness?"

5 He asked them, "How many loaves do you have?" And they said, "Seven."

6 So He commanded the multitude to sit down on the ground. And He took the seven loaves and gave thanks, broke them and gave them to His disciples to set before them; and they set them before the multitude.

7 They also had a few small fish; and having blessed them, He said to set them also before them.

8 So they ate and were filled, and they took up seven large baskets of leftover fragments.

9 Now those who had eaten were about four thousand. And He sent them away,

10 immediately got into the boat with His disciples, and came to the region of Dalmanutha.

11 Then the Pharisees came out and began to dispute with Him, seeking from Him a sign from heaven, testing Him.

12 But He sighed deeply in His spirit, and said, "Why does this generation seek a sign? Assuredly, I say to you, no sign shall be given to this generation."

13 And He left them, and getting into the boat again, departed to the other side.

14 Now the disciples had forgotten to take bread, and they did not have more than one loaf with them in the boat.

15 Then He charged them, saying, "Take heed, beware of the leaven of the Pharisees and the leaven of Herod."

16 And they reasoned among themselves, saying, "It is because we have no bread."

continued with me three days (8:2)—a reflection of the crowd's eagerness to hear Jesus' teaching and experience His healings

How can one satisfy these people with bread (v. 4)—a question underscoring the disciples' spiritual dullness (especially in light of the earlier feeding of the five thousand men)

loaves (v. 5)—flat cakes of bread, easily broken for distribution

large baskets (v. 8)—not "picnic" baskets as in 6:43, but the man-sized baskets commonly used among the Gentiles

sign from heaven (v. 11)—an astronomical miracle

spit on his eyes (v. 23)—an action apparently meant to reassure the sensory-impaired man that a healing was forthcoming

17 But Jesus, being aware of it, said to them, "Why do you reason because you have no bread? Do you not yet perceive nor understand? Is your heart still hardened?

18 Having eyes, do you not see? And having ears, do you not hear? And do you not remember?

19 When I broke the five loaves for the five thousand, how many baskets full of fragments did you take up?" They said to Him, "Twelve."

20 "Also, when I broke the seven for the four thousand, how many large baskets full of fragments did you take up?" And they said, "Seven."

21 So He said to them, "How is it you do not understand?"

22 Then He came to Bethsaida; and they brought a blind man to Him, and begged Him to touch him.

23 So He took the blind man by the hand and led him out of the town. And when He had spit on his eyes and put His hands on him, He asked him if he saw anything.

24 And he looked up and said, "I see men like trees, walking."

25 Then He put His hands on his eyes again and made him look up. And he was restored and saw everyone clearly.

26 Then He sent him away to his house, saying, "Neither go into the town, nor tell anyone in the town."

27 Now Jesus and His disciples went out to the towns of Caesarea Philippi; and on the road He asked His disciples, saying to them, "Who do men say that I am?"

28 So they answered, "John the Baptist; but some say, Elijah; and others, one of the prophets."

29 He said to them, "But who do you say that I am?" Peter answered and said to Him, "You are the Christ."

30 Then He strictly warned them that they should tell no one about Him.

31 And He began to teach them that the Son of Man must suffer many things, and be rejected by the

"You are the Christ" (v. 29)—Peter's confession for the whole group revealed their belief that Christ was the promised Messiah.

tell no one (v. 30)—Jesus knew that broadcasting His identity as Messiah prior to the cross would only lead to greater confusion as the Jewish expectation was for a political/military messiah.

elders and chief priests and scribes, and be killed, and after three days rise again.

32 He spoke this word openly. Then Peter took Him aside and began to rebuke Him.

33 But when He had turned around and looked at His disciples, He rebuked Peter, saying, "Get behind Me, Satan! For you are not mindful of the things of God, but the things of men."

34 When He had called the people to Himself, with His disciples also, He said to them, "Whoever desires to come after Me, let him deny himself, and take up his cross, and follow Me.

35 For whoever desires to save his life will lose it, but whoever loses his life for My sake and the gospel's will save it.

36 For what will it profit a man if he gains the whole world, and loses his own soul?

37 Or what will a man give in exchange for his soul?

38 For whoever is ashamed of Me and My words in this adulterous and sinful generation, of him the Son of Man also will be ashamed when He comes in the glory of His Father with the holy angels."

chief priests (v. 31)—members of the Sanhedrin (council of seventy) and representatives of the twenty-four orders of ordinary priests

scribes (v. 31)—experts in the Old Testament law

Get behind Me, Satan (v. 33)—Unwittingly or not, Peter was serving as Satan's mouth-piece by advocating any path other than the cross.

take up his cross (v. 34)—Christ bids His followers to come and die, certainly to self, and possibly, literally for the gospel.

soul (vv. 36–37)—the real person, who will live forever in heaven or hell

1) Why were the scribes and Pharisees upset with Jesus and His disciples? According to Jesus, what are the dangers of human tradition?

_____

_____

_____

2) Some have accused Jesus of being indifferent, almost rude, to the Syro-Phoenician woman with the sick daughter. What is your impression of what happened in this exchange?

_____

_____

_____

(Verses to consider: Matt. 15:21–28)

3) How are the disciples described in these two chapters? What good qualities do you see? What troubling qualities are present in them?

_____

_____

_____

Going Deeper

To get to the heart of discipleship, compare and contrast Jesus' words in Mark 8:34–38 with Luke 9:23–26.

Exploring the Meaning

4) In our feel-good culture marked by an aversion to commitment, some would say that Jesus' challenge here is not exactly the best way to gain a following.

What does it mean to deny yourself?

_____

_____

To take up your cross daily?

_____

_____

To follow him?

_____

_____

(Verses to consider: Luke 14:25–35; John 12:23–26)

5) In 8:11–13, Jesus refuses to do a trick for the Pharisees who demand some kind of sign. Why does Jesus refuse to make clear His person and power? How does our modern generation compare to the generation described in this passage?

_____

_____

_____

6) Why do you think the disciples were so slow to catch on to Jesus' purpose? What can you learn from their example?

_____

_____

Truth for Today

Christian discipleship strikes a death blow to the self-centered false gospels that are so popular in contemporary Christianity. It leaves no room for the gospel of getting, in which God is considered a type of utilitarian genie who jumps to provide a believer's every whim. It closes the door to the gospel of health and wealth, which asserts that if a believer is not healthy and prosperous he has simply not exercised his divine rights or else does not have enough faith to claim his blessings. It undermines the gospel of self-esteem, self-love, and high self-image, which appeals to man's natural narcissism and prostitutes the spirit of humble brokenness and repentance that marks the gospel of the cross.

To come to Jesus Christ is to receive and to keep on receiving forever. But Jesus, through His direct instruction during His earthly ministry and through His apostles in the rest of the New Testament, repeatedly makes clear that there must be a cross before the crown, suffering before glory, sacrifice before reward. The heart of Christian discipleship is giving before gaining, losing before winning.

Reflecting on the Text

7) The British missionary statesman C. T. Studd once remarked, "If Jesus Christ be God, and He died for me, then no sacrifice can be too great for me to make for Him." How does a life of sacrificial discipleship differ from a life of meaningless religious rituals?

_____

_____

8) As a result of this study, what (if any) human religious traditions do you see that tend to keep you from a closer relationship with Christ?

_____

_____

_____

9) What will "taking up your cross" and "losing your life" involve this week as you follow Christ?

_____

_____

_____

PERSONAL RESPONSE

Write out additional reflections, questions you may have, or a prayer.

_____

_____

_____

_____

_____

_____

_____

_____

_____

_____

_____

_____

_____

_____

_____

_____

_____

7

THE SERVANT PREPARES HIS FOLLOWERS FOR THE FUTURE

Mark 9:1–10:52

DRAWING NEAR

Think of someone you know who is humble and selfless. What actions or attitudes do you see in his or her life?

_____

_____

_____

THE CONTEXT

These two fast-paced chapters record the varied words and actions of Jesus, the Servant-Messiah sent from God. To the casual reader, this passage may seem to be a collection of unrelated, random incidents, but Christ is slowly, deliberately moving toward Jerusalem, the site of His final confrontation with the Jewish religious leaders. Knowing that time is short, Jesus sets about teaching and modeling for His disciples a number of important kingdom truths.

In short order, we see Jesus' true glory revealed in the Transfiguration. He clarified the theological mystery of Elijah's role, cast out a stubborn spirit, predicted, again, His death and resurrection, defined kingdom greatness, identified true spiritual fruit, and warned those who would be stumbling blocks. Furthermore, Jesus teaches on divorce, blesses the children, confronts the rich young ruler, confirms the disciples' rewards, and tries for a third time to prepare the disciples for His death. A careful study of these chapters unveils an intentional effort by Jesus to equip the disciples with the knowledge and skill they will soon need to lead the fledgling church.

KEYS TO THE TEXT

The Transfiguration: Jesus underwent a dramatic change in appearance, so the disciples could behold Him in His glory. The kingdom splendor of Christ revealed at this event was intended as a preview of His majesty to be manifested at His second coming. It is hard to imagine what Jesus looked like when He was transfigured, or changed in form. The Gospel writers speak of His face becoming bright like the sun, and of His clothes being dazzling white. Peter explains that God gave Him honor and glory (2 Pet. 1:17). A cloud overshadowed Jesus during His transfiguration. This has symbolic as well as historical significance. It is a subtle reminder of the Exodus and the appearance of God to Moses on Mount Sinai (Exod. 24), when God also spoke from a cloud. Both Moses and Jesus were accompanied by three companions on their respective experiences. Thus the Old Testament points forward to Christ and His redeeming work. In the Transfiguration God showed clearly that Jesus is His one and only Son, superior even to the two great Old Testament figures, Moses and Elijah. His disciples are to listen to Him. (*Nelson's New Illustrated Bible Dictionary*.)

Kingdom Values—Last Shall Be First: James and John approached Jesus with their request to be seated on His right and left in the kingdom. Ironically, Jesus had just reiterated the importance of humility (see Mark 10:31), and earlier had set a child in their midst as an object lesson about humility. The brothers' error was in desiring *to obtain* the position more than they desired *to be worthy* of such a position. Their ambition was untempered by humility. And Jesus had repeatedly made clear that the highest positions in the kingdom are reserved for the most humble saints on earth. Those who want to be great must first learn to be humble. Christ Himself was the perfection of true humility. Furthermore, His kingdom is advanced by humble service, not by politics, status, power, or dominion.

UNLEASHING THE TEXT

Read 9:1–10:52, noting the key words and definitions next to the passage.

Mark 9:1–10:52 (NKJV)

not taste death till they see the kingdom (v. 1)—until they get a foretaste of Christ's second coming glory, depicted in the Transfiguration, less than one week from this announcement

1 And He said to them, "Assuredly, I say to you that there are some standing here who will not taste death till they see the kingdom of God present with power."

a high mountain (v. 2)—likely Mt. Hermon

transfigured (v. 2)—from a Greek word meaning "to change in form" or "to be transformed"

2 Now after six days Jesus took Peter, James, and John, and led them up on a high mountain apart by themselves; and He was transfigured before them.

shining, exceedingly white (v. 3)—The divine glory emanating from Jesus made even His clothing radiate brilliant white light.

3 His clothes became shining, exceedingly white, like snow, such as no launderer on earth can whiten them.

4 And Elijah appeared to them with Moses, and they were talking with Jesus.

5 *Then Peter answered and said to Jesus, "Rabbi,*
  it is good for us to be here; and let us make three
  tabernacles: one for You, one for Moses, and one for
  Elijah"—

6 *because he did not know what to say, for they were*
  greatly afraid.

7 *And a cloud came and overshadowed them; and*
  a voice came out of the cloud, saying, "This is My
  beloved Son. Hear Him!"

8 *Suddenly, when they had looked around, they saw*
  no one anymore, but only Jesus with themselves.

9 *Now as they came down from the mountain, He*
  commanded them that they should tell no one the
  things they had seen, till the Son of Man had risen
  from the dead.

10 *So they kept this word to themselves, questioning*
  what the rising from the dead meant.

11 *And they asked Him, saying, "Why do the scribes*
  say that Elijah must come first?"

12 *Then He answered and told them, "Indeed, Elijah*
  is coming first and restores all things. And how is it
  written concerning the Son of Man, that He must
  suffer many things and be treated with contempt?

13 *But I say to you that Elijah has also come, and they*
  did to him whatever they wished, as it is written of
  him."

14 *And when He came to the disciples, He saw a great*
  multitude around them, and scribes disputing with
  them.

15 *Immediately, when they saw Him, all the people were*
  greatly amazed, and running to Him, greeted Him.

16 *And He asked the scribes, "What are you discussing*
  with them?"

17 *Then one of the crowd answered and said, "Teacher,*
  I brought You my son, who has a mute spirit.

18 *And wherever it seizes him, it throws him down; he*
  foams at the mouth, gnashes his teeth, and becomes
  rigid. So I spoke to Your disciples, that they should
  cast it out, but they could not."

Elijah . . . with Moses (v. 4)— symbolic of the Prophets (Elijah) and the Law (Moses), the two great divisions of the Old Testament

let us make three tabernacles (v. 5)—Peter may have thought the millennial kingdom was about to be inaugurated.

a cloud (v. 7)—the Shekinah glory cloud, symbolic of God's presence

tell no one (v. 9)—Christ wanted the messianic mission (to conquer sin and death, not the Romans) to be evident and clear.

Elijah must come first . . . Elijah has also come (vv. 11–13)—The familiar prophecies of Elijah's coming had been fulfilled in John the Baptist.

they could not (v. 18)—surprising in view of the power and authority granted them by Christ

I believe; help my unbelief (v. 24)—a candid admission of imperfect faith and a plea for divine help

This kind (v. 29)—Apparently some demons are more powerful and obstinate than others.

fasting (v. 29)—Most ancient manuscripts omit this word.

19 *He answered him and said, "O faithless generation, how long shall I be with you? How long shall I bear with you? Bring him to Me."*

20 *Then they brought him to Him. And when he saw Him, immediately the spirit convulsed him, and he fell on the ground and wallowed, foaming at the mouth.*

21 *So He asked his father, "How long has this been happening to him?" And he said, "From childhood.*

22 *And often he has thrown him both into the fire and into the water to destroy him. But if You can do anything, have compassion on us and help us."*

23 *Jesus said to him, "If you can believe, all things are possible to him who believes."*

24 *Immediately the father of the child cried out and said with tears, "Lord, I believe; help my unbelief!"*

25 *When Jesus saw that the people came running together, He rebuked the unclean spirit, saying to it, "Deaf and dumb spirit, I command you, come out of him and enter him no more!"*

26 *Then the spirit cried out, convulsed him greatly, and came out of him. And he became as one dead, so that many said, "He is dead."*

27 *But Jesus took him by the hand and lifted him up, and he arose.*

28 *And when He had come into the house, His disciples asked Him privately, "Why could we not cast it out?"*

29 *So He said to them, "This kind can come out by nothing but prayer and fasting."*

30 *Then they departed from there and passed through Galilee, and He did not want anyone to know it.*

31 *For He taught His disciples and said to them, "The Son of Man is being betrayed into the hands of men, and they will kill Him. And after He is killed, He will rise the third day."*

32 *But they did not understand this saying, and were afraid to ask Him.*

33 *Then He came to Capernaum. And when He was in the house He asked them, "What was it you*

disputed among yourselves on the road?"

34 But they kept silent, for on the road they had disputed among themselves who would be the greatest.

35 And He sat down, called the twelve, and said to them, "If anyone desires to be first, he shall be last of all and servant of all."

36 Then He took a little child and set him in the midst of them. And when He had taken him in His arms, He said to them,

37 "Whoever receives one of these little children in My name receives Me; and whoever receives Me, receives not Me but Him who sent Me."

38 Now John answered Him, saying, "Teacher, we saw someone who does not follow us casting out demons in Your name, and we forbade him because he does not follow us."

39 But Jesus said, "Do not forbid him, for no one who works a miracle in My name can soon afterward speak evil of Me.

40 For he who is not against us is on our side.

41 For whoever gives you a cup of water to drink in My name, because you belong to Christ, assuredly, I say to you, he will by no means lose his reward.

42 "But whoever causes one of these little ones who believe in Me to stumble, it would be better for him if a millstone were hung around his neck, and he were thrown into the sea.

43 If your hand causes you to sin, cut it off. It is better for you to enter into life maimed, rather than having two hands, to go to hell, into the fire that shall never be quenched—

44 where 'Their worm does not die And the fire is not quenched.'

45 And if your foot causes you to sin, cut it off. It is better for you to enter life lame, rather than having two feet, to be cast into hell, into the fire that shall never be quenched—

46 where 'Their worm does not die And the fire is not quenched.'

they kept silent (v. 34)—likely out of conviction and embarrassment

desires to be first, he shall be last (v. 35)—The disciples' concepts of greatness and leadership, drawn from their culture, were exactly backwards.

a little child (v. 36)—The Greek word suggests an infant or toddler.

to stumble (v. 42)—to lead into sin or cause to fall into sin

cut it off (v. 43)—a figurative statement, since no amount of physical mutilation can deal with the root of sin, that is, a wayward heart

came . . . testing Him (v. 2)—
By publicly discrediting Jesus,
the Jewish leaders hoped to
turn popular sentiment against
Him and thereby make it easier
to dispose of Him.

Moses . . . permitted divorce
(v. 4)—The law permitted, but
did not command or condone
divorce in the case of flagrant,
unrepentant sexual immorality.

47 *And if your eye causes you to sin, pluck it out. It is better for you to enter the kingdom of God with one eye, rather than having two eyes, to be cast into hell fire—*

48 *where 'Their worm does not die And the fire is not quenched.'*

49 *"For everyone will be seasoned with fire, and every sacrifice will be seasoned with salt.*

50 *Salt is good, but if the salt loses its flavor, how will you season it? Have salt in yourselves, and have peace with one another."*

10:1 *Then He arose from there and came to the region of Judea by the other side of the Jordan. And multitudes gathered to Him again, and as He was accustomed, He taught them again.*

2 *The Pharisees came and asked Him, "Is it lawful for a man to divorce his wife?" testing Him.*

3 *And He answered and said to them, "What did Moses command you?"*

4 *They said, "Moses permitted a man to write a certificate of divorce, and to dismiss her."*

5 *And Jesus answered and said to them, "Because of the hardness of your heart he wrote you this precept.*

6 *But from the beginning of the creation, God 'made them male and female.'*

7 *'For this reason a man shall leave his father and mother and be joined to his wife,*

8 *and the two shall become one flesh'; so then they are no longer two, but one flesh.*

9 *Therefore what God has joined together, let not man separate."*

10 *In the house His disciples also asked Him again about the same matter.*

11 *So He said to them, "Whoever divorces his wife and marries another commits adultery against her.*

12 *And if a woman divorces her husband and marries another, she commits adultery."*

13 *Then they brought little children to Him, that He might touch them; but the disciples rebuked those who brought them.*

14 *But when Jesus saw it, He was greatly displeased and said to them, "Let the little children come to Me, and do not forbid them; for of such is the kingdom of God.*

15 *Assuredly, I say to you, whoever does not receive the kingdom of God as a little child will by no means enter it."*

16 *And He took them up in His arms, laid His hands on them, and blessed them.*

17 *Now as He was going out on the road, one came running, knelt before Him, and asked Him, "Good Teacher, what shall I do that I may inherit eternal life?"*

18 *So Jesus said to him, "Why do you call Me good? No one is good but One, that is, God.*

19 *You know the commandments: 'Do not commit adultery,' 'Do not murder,' 'Do not steal,' 'Do not bear false witness,' 'Do not defraud,' 'Honor your father and your mother.'"*

20 *And he answered and said to Him, "Teacher, all these things I have kept from my youth."*

21 *Then Jesus, looking at him, loved him, and said to him, "One thing you lack: Go your way, sell whatever you have and give to the poor, and you will have treasure in heaven; and come, take up the cross, and follow Me."*

22 *But he was sad at this word, and went away sorrowful, for he had great possessions.*

23 *Then Jesus looked around and said to His disciples, "How hard it is for those who have riches to enter the kingdom of God!"*

24 *And the disciples were astonished at His words. But Jesus answered again and said to them, "Children, how hard it is for those who trust in riches to enter the kingdom of God!*

25 *It is easier for a camel to go through the eye of a needle than for a rich man to enter the kingdom of God."*

26 *And they were greatly astonished, saying among themselves, "Who then can be saved?"*

what shall I do (v. 17)—Steeped in the legalism of the day, this young man was looking for a deed he could accomplish so as to secure eternal life.

Why do you call me good? (v.18)—not a denial of deity, but an implied affirmation of it

all these things I have kept (v. 20)—externally, perhaps, but not in terms of internal attitudes and motives

sell whatever you have (v. 21)—not a way to be saved, but an attempt to expose the man's unadmitted sinfulness

camel . . . eye of a needle (v. 25)—a colloquialism indicating impossibility

up to Jerusalem (v. 32)—because the city was and is literally some 2,500 feet above sea level

27 But Jesus looked at them and said, "With men it is impossible, but not with God; for with God all things are possible."

28 Then Peter began to say to Him, "See, we have left all and followed You."

29 So Jesus answered and said, "Assuredly, I say to you, there is no one who has left house or brothers or sisters or father or mother or wife or children or lands, for My sake and the gospel's,

30 who shall not receive a hundredfold now in this time—houses and brothers and sisters and mothers and children and lands, with persecutions—and in the age to come, eternal life.

31 But many who are first will be last, and the last first."

32 Now they were on the road, going up to Jerusalem, and Jesus was going before them; and they were amazed. And as they followed they were afraid. Then He took the twelve aside again and began to tell them the things that would happen to Him:

33 "Behold, we are going up to Jerusalem, and the Son of Man will be betrayed to the chief priests and to the scribes; and they will condemn Him to death and deliver Him to the Gentiles;

34 and they will mock Him, and scourge Him, and spit on Him, and kill Him. And the third day He will rise again."

35 Then James and John, the sons of Zebedee, came to Him, saying, "Teacher, we want You to do for us whatever we ask."

36 And He said to them, "What do you want Me to do for you?"

37 They said to Him, "Grant us that we may sit, one on Your right hand and the other on Your left, in Your glory."

the cup . . . the baptism (v. 38)—endure suffering and death as Jesus would face (Jesus tells them they will indeed drink the same cup and be baptized with the same baptism).

38 But Jesus said to them, "You do not know what you ask. Are you able to drink the cup that I drink, and be baptized with the baptism that I am baptized with?"

39 They said to Him, "We are able." So Jesus said to them, "You will indeed drink the cup that I drink,

and with the baptism I am baptized with you will
be baptized;

40 but to sit on My right hand and on My left is not
Mine to give, but it is for those for whom it is
prepared."

41 And when the ten heard it, they began to be greatly
displeased with James and John.

42 But Jesus called them to Himself and said to them,
"You know that those who are considered rulers
over the Gentiles lord it over them, and their great
ones exercise authority over them.

43 Yet it shall not be so among you; but whoever desires
to become great among you shall be your servant.

44 And whoever of you desires to be first shall be slave
of all.

45 For even the Son of Man did not come to be served,
but to serve, and to give His life a ransom for
many."

46 Now they came to Jericho. As He went out of Jericho
with His disciples and a great multitude, blind
Bartimaeus, the son of Timaeus, sat by the road
begging.

47 And when he heard that it was Jesus of Nazareth, he
began to cry out and say, "Jesus, Son of David, have
mercy on me!"

48 Then many warned him to be quiet; but he cried out
all the more, "Son of David, have mercy on me!"

49 So Jesus stood still and commanded him to be called.
Then they called the blind man, saying to him, "Be
of good cheer. Rise, He is calling you."

50 And throwing aside his garment, he rose and came
to Jesus.

51 So Jesus answered and said to him, "What do you
want Me to do for you?" The blind man said to
Him, "Rabboni, that I may receive my sight."

52 Then Jesus said to him, "Go your way; your faith
has made you well." And immediately he received
his sight and followed Jesus on the road.

not Mine to give (v. 40)—Kingdom rewards will be bestowed according to the sovereign will of God.

not so among you (v. 43)—Domineering, worldly leadership has no place in the church.

ransom (v. 45)—the price paid to free a slave or prisoner; hence Christ's substitutionary death satisfied the demands of God's holy wrath against sin

1) What effect did the Transfiguration have on Peter, James, and John? What did this event reveal about Christ?

_____

_____

_____

2) What specific lessons did Jesus teach His followers about servanthood in this passage?

_____

_____

_____

3) Twice in this passage Mark records Jesus interacting with children. What insights and truths do you glean from these interactions?

_____

_____

_____

Going Deeper

Read Genesis 2:21–25, God's original design for marriage. Compare it with what Jesus says in Mark 10:1–12 about divorce.

Exploring the Meaning

4) From Genesis 2:21–25, what is the purpose of marriage?

_____

_____

5) What further light does Jesus' teaching shed on marriage and divorce?

_____

_____

_____

(Verses to consider: Mal. 2:16; Matt. 19:1–9; Eph. 5:22–33)

6) Based on Jesus' encounter with the "rich young ruler," in what ways can material wealth be detrimental?

_____

_____

_____

_____

(Verses to consider: Prov. 30:8–9; Luke 8:14; 16:13)

7) What does it mean that Christ gave His life as "a ransom for many" (10:45)? Define this in your own words.

_____

_____

_____

_____

(Verses to consider: 1 Cor. 6:20; Gal. 3:13; Eph. 1:7; Tit. 2:14; 1 Pet. 1:18–19)

TRUTH FOR TODAY

The cost of true greatness is humble, selfless, sacrificial service. The Christian who desires to be great and first in the kingdom is the one who is willing to serve in the hard place, the uncomfortable place, the lonely place, the demanding place, the place where he is not appreciated and may even be persecuted. Knowing that time is short and eternity long, he is willing to spend and be spent. He is willing to work for excellence without becoming proud, to withstand criticism without becoming bitter, to be misjudged without becoming defensive, and to withstand suffering without succumbing to self-pity.

REFLECTING ON THE TEXT

8) Why do you think Christ's teaching of the "first shall be last; last shall be first" is so hard to swallow for most people?

_____

_____

_____

_____

9) Given the performance of the disciples in the various incidents recorded in these chapters, how ready for leadership were they?

_____

_____

_____

10) With what character in this passage do you most relate (the disciples who had just witnessed the glory of Christ; the parent of a child in trouble; the disciples confused over what lay ahead; the people scrambling for a position; the young ruler with tremendous wealth; Bartimaeus, fervently seeking help)? Explain why.

_____

_____

_____

11) What specific change or action do you need to take in your faith walk as a result of this lesson? Find a Christian friend to pray with you in this matter and hold you accountable.

_____

_____

_____

PERSONAL RESPONSE

Write out additional reflections, questions you may have, or a prayer.

_____

_____

_____

_____

_____

_____

_____

8

THE SERVANT'S CORONATION
Mark 11:1–33

DRAWING NEAR

What new truths about Jesus have you discovered thus far in this study of the book of Mark? Has anything about Him surprised you? Bothered you? Comforted you?

_____

_____

_____

Take some time to reflect on who Jesus is, and thank God for sending His Son.

THE CONTEXT

Hurtling toward a dramatic conclusion, Mark portrays the most significant coronation the world has yet seen, but a coronation unlike any other in history. This is a coronation of a true King—but without pomp, splendor, and pageantry.

After arriving in Jerusalem, Jesus the Servant shows that He has a divine mission. For the second time in His ministry, He makes a public stir by cleansing the temple of its moneychangers and merchants. Then He underscores this judgment of hypocritical religion by cursing a nearby fig tree that has leaves but no fruit. When His disciples wonder about this action, Jesus uses the opportunity to teach them about faith, prayer, and forgiveness. Again confronted by the Jewish religious leaders about His behavior, Jesus puts them on the defensive, insuring a final confrontation with them.

KEYS TO THE TEXT

The Temple: The New Testament uses two words for *temple.* One of these words refers to the collection of buildings that made up the temple in Jerusalem, while the other usually refers to the sanctuary of the temple. Jesus related to the temple in four distinct ways. First, as a pious Jew who was zealous for the Lord, Jesus showed respect for the temple. He referred to it as "the house of God" and "My Father's house." Second, Jesus' zeal led Him to purge the temple of the moneychangers and to weep over it as He reflected on its coming destruction. Third, because He was the Son of God incarnate, Jesus taught that He was greater than the temple. Finally, Jesus taught that the church is the new, eschatological temple. At Jesus' death, the curtain of the temple was torn from top to bottom. By His death, Jesus opened a new way into the presence of God. No longer was the temple in Jerusalem to be the place where people worshiped God. From now on they would worship Him "in spirit and truth" (John 4:21–24). (*Nelson's New Illustrated Bible Dictionary*)

UNLEASHING THE TEXT

Read 11:1–33, noting the key words and definitions next to the passage.

Bethany (v. 1)—the hometown of Mary, Martha, and Lazarus

colt (v. 2)—a young donkey, in accordance with Old Testament prophecies of this event

spread their clothes (v. 8)—an ancient practice when welcoming a new king

leafy branches (v. 8)—palm branches symbolizing joy and salvation

Hosanna (v. 9)—literally, "save now"; used here as a form of welcome

Mark 11:1–33 (NKJV)

1 *Now when they drew near Jerusalem, to Bethphage and Bethany, at the Mount of Olives, He sent two of His disciples;*

2 *and He said to them, "Go into the village opposite you; and as soon as you have entered it you will find a colt tied, on which no one has sat. Loose it and bring it.*

3 *And if anyone says to you, 'Why are you doing this?' say, 'The Lord has need of it,' and immediately he will send it here."*

4 *So they went their way, and found the colt tied by the door outside on the street, and they loosed it.*

5 *But some of those who stood there said to them, "What are you doing, loosing the colt?"*

6 *And they spoke to them just as Jesus had commanded. So they let them go.*

7 *Then they brought the colt to Jesus and threw their clothes on it, and He sat on it.*

8 *And many spread their clothes on the road, and others cut down leafy branches from the trees and spread them on the road.*

9 *Then those who went before and those who followed cried out, saying: "Hosanna! 'Blessed is He who comes in the name of the Lord!'*

10 *Blessed is the kingdom of our father David That comes in the name of the Lord! Hosanna in the highest!"*

11 *And Jesus went into Jerusalem and into the temple. So when He had looked around at all things, as the hour was already late, He went out to Bethany with the twelve.*

12 *Now the next day, when they had come out from Bethany, He was hungry.*

13 *And seeing from afar a fig tree having leaves, He went to see if perhaps He would find something on it. When He came to it, He found nothing but leaves, for it was not the season for figs.*

14 *In response Jesus said to it, "Let no one eat fruit from you ever again." And His disciples heard it.*

15 *So they came to Jerusalem. Then Jesus went into the temple and began to drive out those who bought and sold in the temple, and overturned the tables of the money changers and the seats of those who sold doves.*

16 *And He would not allow anyone to carry wares through the temple.*

17 *Then He taught, saying to them, "Is it not written, 'My house shall be called a house of prayer for all nations'? But you have made it a 'den of thieves.'"*

18 *And the scribes and chief priests heard it and sought how they might destroy Him; for they feared Him, because all the people were astonished at His teaching.*

19 *When evening had come, He went out of the city.*

20 *Now in the morning, as they passed by, they saw the fig tree dried up from the roots.*

21 *And Peter, remembering, said to Him, "Rabbi, look! The fig tree which You cursed has withered away."*

22 *So Jesus answered and said to them, "Have faith in God.*

23 *For assuredly, I say to you, whoever says to this mountain, 'Be removed and be cast into the sea,' and does not doubt in his heart, but believes that those things he says will be done, he will have whatever he says.*

24 *Therefore I say to you, whatever things you ask when you pray, believe that you receive them, and you will have them.*

temple (v. 11)—not the inner sanctum, but the entire complex of courtyards and buildings

fig tree having leaves . . . not the season for figs (v. 13)—Figs normally grew along with the leaves, but this tree strangely had none; despite being ahead of schedule with foliage, it bore no fruit.

money changers (v. 15)—merchants who set up shop in the temple courts to exchange foreign money (that is, Greek, Roman) for the Jewish or Tyrian coins required to purchase sacrificial animals; a fee of 10–12 percent often would be charged for this simple service

carry wares through the temple (v. 16)—Apparently people were irreverently using the temple as a shortcut.

for all nations (v. 17)—The temple's court of the Gentiles shows God's love for the whole world, but their designated place for worship was cluttered with the trappings of commercialism.

went out of the city (v. 19)—Jesus left the city the first three days of Passion Week (probably for Bethany) about sunset when the crowds had thinned and as the city gates were closing.

this mountain . . . into the seas (v. 23)—an expression, literally, "rooter up of mountains," related to a common metaphor used in the Jewish literature of rabbis who could solve great problems and seemingly do the impossible; Jesus' idea is that believers who sincerely trust God will see His mighty power

25 *"And whenever you stand praying, if you have anything against anyone, forgive him, that your Father in heaven may also forgive you your trespasses.*

26 *But if you do not forgive, neither will your Father in heaven forgive your trespasses."*

27 *Then they came again to Jerusalem. And as He was walking in the temple, the chief priests, the scribes, and the elders came to Him.*

28 *And they said to Him, "By what authority are You doing these things? And who gave You this authority to do these things?"*

29 *But Jesus answered and said to them, "I also will ask you one question; then answer Me, and I will tell you by what authority I do these things:*

30 *The baptism of John—was it from heaven or from men? Answer Me."*

31 *And they reasoned among themselves, saying, "If we say, 'From heaven,' He will say, 'Why then did you not believe him?'*

32 *But if we say, 'From men' "—they feared the people, for all counted John to have been a prophet indeed.*

33 *So they answered and said to Jesus, "We do not know." And Jesus answered and said to them, "Neither will I tell you by what authority I do these things."*

these things (v. 28)—primarily the clearing of the temple, but in a broader sense, all the actions of His ministry

from heaven or from men? (v. 30)—Jesus put the leaders on the defensive by requiring them to make a public statement about John's ministry (and, indirectly, His own).

1) What details stand out to you in this account of the triumphal entry of Christ into Jerusalem? Describe the mood of this event.

_____

_____

2) If someone commented, "I think it's weird that Jesus cursed that fig tree!" how would you respond? How would you explain Christ's actions?

_____

_____

_____

3) What did Jesus do to cleanse the temple? Why was He so angered by what He saw?

_____

_____

_____

4) What more do you learn about Jesus from how He responded this time to the chief priests and scribes (11:27–33)?

_____

_____

_____

Going Deeper

Read Psalm 118. In Old Testament times, this psalm was often recited by Jewish pilgrims as they made their way to Jerusalem, the Holy City. Part of it was shouted by the crowd as Jesus entered Jerusalem on the borrowed colt.

Exploring the Meaning

5) How does Psalm 118 enhance your sense of the scene described in Mark 11, as Jesus made His way into the city?

_____

_____

_____

6) Following Christ's explanation of the withered fig tree, the disciples received a lesson in faith and prayer. What does it mean that our faith "can move mountains"? What does it not mean?

_____

_____

_____

7) What motivated the Jewish religious leaders to plot and scheme against Christ to the degree that they did? Why do you think they continued to hate him so much?

_____

_____

_____

Truth for Today

The great problem with society is not injustice, inequity, crime, or even immorality—pervasive and destructive as those evils might be. Society's evil of evils has always been its abandonment of God. And it is as true today as it was in ancient Israel that the people of God must themselves be revived and renewed before they can be His instruments for changing the world around them.

Reflecting on the Text

8) If Jesus visited some of our modern-day churches or religious activities, do you think He would be pleased or disgusted? Why? What aspects of the North American church might offend Him?

_____

_____

_____

9) Does your life contain the appearance of Christianity, but without the proof? In what ways do you need Jesus to revive and renew you?

_____

_____

_____

10) For what two "impossible" things do you need to trust God today? How can you demonstrate faith?

_____

_____

_____

Personal Response

Write out additional reflections, questions you may have, or a prayer.

ADDITIONAL NOTES

9

THE SERVANT CONFRONTED AND QUESTIONED
Mark 12:1–44

DRAWING NEAR

Imagine that Jesus is sitting here with you. If you could say anything or ask Him any question right now, what would it be?

_____

_____

_____

THE CONTEXT

The Jewish religious establishment resented Jesus because He exposed their pride, hypocrisy, and self-righteousness. They envied His great popularity with the people, and were incensed at His claim to be the Messiah and the Son of God, a claim that in their eyes was blatant blasphemy. Now, after a scathing parable told by Jesus to highlight their murderous motives (1–12), the leaders are infuriated and even more determined to find a way to kill Jesus. They try to trap Him with a series of tricky political and theological conundrums. Jesus' brilliant responses silence His critics, and He then fires back a question or two of His own. Following another assertion of Messiahship, Christ publicly condemns the hypocrisy of the scribes.

KEYS TO THE TEXT

Parable: A short, simple story designed to communicate a spiritual truth, religious principle, or moral lesson. In this parable of the vineyard owner, Jesus alludes to Isaiah 5:1–2, which would have been familiar to the Jewish leaders. The "vineyard" is a common symbol for the Jewish nation in Scripture. Here the landowner, representing God, developed the vineyard with great care, then leased it to vinedressers, representing the Jewish leaders. The vinedressers were greedy; because they wanted the entire harvest and the vineyard for themselves and would stop at nothing to achieve that end, they plotted to kill the owner's son. Because Jesus had achieved such a following, the Jewish leaders believed the only way to maintain their position and power over the people was to kill Him.

The Great Commandment: First in the list of all that was essential for the Jew was unreserved, wholehearted commitment expressed in love to God. Since this relationship of love for God could not be represented in any material way as with idols, it had to be demonstrated in obedience to God's law in daily life. Jesus quoted the Jewish confession of faith known as Shema during this dispute with the scribes in 12:28–30. The Shema begins, "Hear, O Israel: The LORD our God, the LORD is one!" (Deut. 6:4). The complete Shema is found in three passages from the Old Testament: Numbers 15:37–41, Deuteronomy 6:4–9 and 11:13–21. These verses make up one of the most ancient features of worship among the Jewish people. (*Nelson's New Illustrated Bible Dictionary*)

UNLEASHING THE TEXT

Read 12:1–44, noting the key words and definitions next to the passage.

Mark 12:1–44 (NKJV)

hedge (v. 1)—literally, "a fence"; maybe a stone wall or hedge of briars built for protection

leased it (v. 1)—The renters would pay a certain percentage for the right to farm.

vintage-time (v. 2)—harvest time

1 Then He began to speak to them in parables: "A man planted a vineyard and set a hedge around it, dug a place for the wine vat and built a tower. And he leased it to vinedressers and went into a far country.

2 Now at vintage-time he sent a servant to the vinedressers, that he might receive some of the fruit of the vineyard from the vinedressers.

3 And they took him and beat him and sent him away empty-handed.

4 Again he sent them another servant, and at him they threw stones, wounded him in the head, and sent him away shamefully treated.

5 And again he sent another, and him they killed; and many others, beating some and killing some.

son, his beloved (v. 6)—representative of Jesus Christ

6 Therefore still having one son, his beloved, he also sent him to them last, saying, 'They will respect my son.'

the inheritance will be ours (v. 7)—Greed caused them to become murderous (much as the jealous, prideful religious leaders would kill Christ).

7 But those vinedressers said among themselves, 'This is the heir. Come, let us kill him, and the inheritance will be ours.'

8 So they took him and killed him and cast him out of the vineyard.

give the vineyard to others (v. 9)—fulfilled in the establishment of the church

9 "Therefore what will the owner of the vineyard do? He will come and destroy the vinedressers, and give the vineyard to others.

10 *Have you not even read this Scripture: 'The stone which the builders rejected Has become the chief cornerstone.*

11 *This was the Lord's doing, And it is marvelous in our eyes'?"*

12 *And they sought to lay hands on Him, but feared the multitude, for they knew He had spoken the parable against them. So they left Him and went away.*

13 *Then they sent to Him some of the Pharisees and the Herodians, to catch Him in His words.*

14 *When they had come, they said to Him, "Teacher, we know that You are true, and care about no one; for You do not regard the person of men, but teach the way of God in truth. Is it lawful to pay taxes to Caesar, or not?*

15 *Shall we pay, or shall we not pay?" But He, knowing their hypocrisy, said to them, "Why do you test Me? Bring Me a denarius that I may see it."*

16 *So they brought it. And He said to them, "Whose image and inscription is this?" They said to Him, "Caesar's."*

17 *And Jesus answered and said to them, "Render to Caesar the things that are Caesar's, and to God the things that are God's." And they marveled at Him.*

18 *Then some Sadducees, who say there is no resurrection, came to Him; and they asked Him, saying:*

19 *"Teacher, Moses wrote to us that if a man's brother dies, and leaves his wife behind, and leaves no children, his brother should take his wife and raise up offspring for his brother.*

20 *Now there were seven brothers. The first took a wife; and dying, he left no offspring.*

21 *And the second took her, and he died; nor did he leave any offspring. And the third likewise.*

22 *So the seven had her and left no offspring. Last of all the woman died also.*

23 *Therefore, in the resurrection, when they rise, whose wife will she be? For all seven had her as wife."*

spoken the parable against them (v. 12)—The religious leaders understood the parable as aimed at their actions, but it only enraged them more.

Herodians (v. 13)—a political party backing Herod Antipas, Rome's puppet ruler

regard the person of men (v. 14)—Do not show favoritism.

Render to Caesar (v. 17)—Literally, "pay" or "give back," implying that citizens are indebted to their government authorities and taxpaying is not optional.

Sadducees (v. 18)—the most wealthy, influential, and aristocratic of all the Jewish sects

You are . . . greatly mistaken (v.
27)—Christ flatly accused the
Sadducees of being wrong on
the subject of resurrection.

**Which is the first command-
ment of all?** (v. 28)—The
Pharisees had codified the
Mosaic Law into 613 separate
commandments; a frequent
theological debate concerned
which of all these laws should
take precedence.

the second, like it (v. 31)—Jesus
linked love for God with love
for humankind.

not far from the kingdom (v.
34)—A compliment, but also a
challenge to love and obey the
One who alone can grant en-
trance to the kingdom.

24 *Jesus answered and said to them, "Are you not
therefore mistaken, because you do not know the
Scriptures nor the power of God?*

25 *For when they rise from the dead, they neither
marry nor are given in marriage, but are like angels
in heaven.*

26 *But concerning the dead, that they rise, have you
not read in the book of Moses, in the burning bush
passage, how God spoke to him, saying, 'I am the
God of Abraham, the God of Isaac, and the God of
Jacob'?*

27 *He is not the God of the dead, but the God of the
living. You are therefore greatly mistaken."*

28 *Then one of the scribes came, and having heard
them reasoning together, perceiving that He had
answered them well, asked Him, "Which is the first
commandment of all?"*

29 *Jesus answered him, "The first of all the
commandments is: 'Hear, O Israel, the Lord our
God, the Lord is one.*

30 *And you shall love the Lord your God with all your
heart, with all your soul, with all your mind, and with
all your strength.' This is the first commandment.*

31 *And the second, like it, is this: 'You shall love
your neighbor as yourself.' There is no other
commandment greater than these."*

32 *So the scribe said to Him, "Well said, Teacher. You
have spoken the truth, for there is one God, and
there is no other but He.*

33 *And to love Him with all the heart, with all the
understanding, with all the soul, and with all the
strength, and to love one's neighbor as oneself, is more
than all the whole burnt offerings and sacrifices."*

34 *Now when Jesus saw that he answered wisely, He
said to him, "You are not far from the kingdom of
God." But after that no one dared question Him.*

35 *Then Jesus answered and said, while He taught in
the temple, "How is it that the scribes say that the
Christ is the Son of David?*

36 *For David himself said by the Holy Spirit: 'The Lord said to my Lord, "Sit at My right hand, Till I make Your enemies Your footstool."*

37 *Therefore David himself calls Him 'Lord'; how is He then his Son?" And the common people heard Him gladly.*

38 *Then He said to them in His teaching, "Beware of the scribes, who desire to go around in long robes, love greetings in the marketplaces,*

39 *the best seats in the synagogues, and the best places at feasts,*

40 *who devour widows' houses, and for a pretense make long prayers. These will receive greater condemnation."*

41 *Now Jesus sat opposite the treasury and saw how the people put money into the treasury. And many who were rich put in much.*

42 *Then one poor widow came and threw in two mites, which make a quadrans.*

43 *So He called His disciples to Himself and said to them, "Assuredly, I say to you that this poor widow has put in more than all those who have given to the treasury;*

44 *for they all put in out of their abundance, but she out of her poverty put in all that she had, her whole livelihood."*

David himself calls Him "Lord" (v. 37)—David's reference to one of his descendants as "Lord" implies deity. Thus the Son of David was also the Son of God, the Messiah.

Beware (v. 38)—Literally, "to see" or "to watch"; carrying the idea of guarding against the evil influence of the scribes.

devour widows' houses (v. 40)—a reference to unscrupulous advice-giving and estate-planning by some scribes.

treasury (v. 41)—thirteen trumpet shaped receptacles positioned along the walls of the court of the women

mites (v. 42)—copper coins, each worth about an eighth of a cent

her whole livelihood (v. 44)—literally, "all she had to live on," that is, a truly sacrificial gift

1) Who do the various characters in the parable of the vineyard owner represent? What was the Jewish response to this story by Christ?

_____

_____

_____

2) The question concerning taxes was an attempt to get Jesus to say or do what? What do you think his answer means?

_____

_____

_____

3) What was Jesus' ingenious response to the trick question about the resurrection?

_____

_____

_____

_____

GOING DEEPER

The first Gospel of Matthew includes a more detailed denunciation by Christ of the Jewish religious leaders. Read through Jesus' strong, sobering words in Matthew 23.

EXPLORING THE MEANING

4) According to Matthew 23, why were the scribes and Pharisees unfit to be spiritual leaders of Israel?

_____

_____

_____

_____

5) How can you "render to Caesar the things that are Caesar's"? What would that mean for us today?

_____

_____

_____

_____

(Verses to consider: Rom. 13:1–7; 1 Pet. 2:13–17)

6) Why did the poor widow catch Jesus' eye? What message was Jesus attempting to convey to His disciples through this incident?

_____

_____

_____

TRUTH FOR TODAY

The person who truly loves the Lord with all his heart and soul and mind is the person who trusts Him and obeys Him. That person demonstrates his love by meditating on God's glory (Psalm 18:1–3), trusting in God's divine power (Psalm 31:23), seeking fellowship with God (Psalm 63:1–8), loving God's law (Psalm 119:165), being sensitive to how God feels (Psalm 69:9), loving what God loves (Psalm 119:72, 97, 103), loving whom God loves (1 John 5:1), hating what God hates (Psalm 97:10), grieving over sin (Matthew 26:75), rejecting the world (1 John 2:15), longing to be with Christ (2 Timothy 4:8), and obeying God wholeheartedly (John 14:21).

REFLECTING ON THE TEXT

7) How well are you living out "the Great Commandment" (12:29–30)? What does it mean to love God with heart, soul, mind, and strength?

_____

_____

_____

_____

8) As you ponder the tremendous sacrifice of the poor widow, what needs to change in your life when it comes to giving back to God?

_____

_____

_____

_____

(Verses to consider: Prov. 3:9–10; Mal. 1:6–8; Matt. 10:8; 2 Cor. 9:6–8)

9) What two spiritual leaders or mentors have faithfully ministered to you and provided an example of godliness for you? What can you do this week to express your gratitude for the impact they've had in your life?

_____

_____

_____

_____

Personal Response

Write out additional reflections, questions you may have, or a prayer.

_____

_____

_____

_____

_____

_____

_____

_____

_____

_____

_____

_____

_____

_____

_____

_____

_____

_____

_____

_____

_____

_____

_____

_____

_____

_____

_____

10

THE SERVANT REVEALS THINGS TO COME

Mark 13:1–37

DRAWING NEAR

When you think about the future, what causes you to worry? What causes you to anticipate the future?

_____

_____

_____

When you think about Jesus coming again, what images come to mind?

_____

_____

_____

THE CONTEXT

It is the final week of Christ's earthly life and ministry. The Son of Man has entered Jerusalem to the glad shouts of the masses but also to the anger and consternation of the Jewish religious leaders. By driving the moneychangers and merchants from the temple and publicly rebuking the scribes and Pharisees, Jesus set Himself on a collision course with the cross. But there are still questions to be answered and lessons to be taught. And so Jesus seizes the opportunity to give His followers insight into things to come.

This sermon by Jesus (chapter 13) is commonly known as the Olivet Discourse because Jesus delivered it on the Mount of Olives just east of the temple, across the Kidron Valley. Jesus' prediction of the coming destruction of the temple prompted a question from the disciples about the character of the end times (vv. 1–4). The remainder of the passage (vv. 5–37) is Jesus' response to their question as He describes His second coming at the end of the present age. All who are intrigued or confused by what the future holds will find this to be a fascinating study.

KEYS TO THE TEXT

Eschatology: The study of what will happen when all things are consummated at the end of history, particularly centering on the event known as the second coming of Christ. The word comes from two Greek words, *eschatos* (last) and *logos* (study)—thus its definition as "the study of last things." (*Nelson's New Illustrated Bible Dictionary*)

Second Coming: Christ's future return to the earth at the end of the present age. Although the Bible explicitly speaks of Christ's appearance as a "second time," the phrase "second coming" occurs nowhere in the New Testament. Many passages, however, speak of His return. In the New Testament alone it is referred to over 300 times. The night before His crucifixion, Jesus told His apostles that He would return (John 14:3). When Jesus ascended into heaven, two angels appeared to His followers, saying that He would return in the same manner as they had seen Him go (Acts 1:11). The New Testament is filled with expectancy of His coming, even as Christians should be today. (*Nelson's New Illustrated Bible Dictionary*)

UNLEASHING THE TEXT

Read 13:1–37, noting the key words and definitions next to the passage.

Mark 13:1–37 (NKJV)

what manner of stones and what buildings (v. 1)—a statement of admiration at the temple complex's grandeur and size

1 *Then as He went out of the temple, one of His disciples said to Him, "Teacher, see what manner of stones and what buildings are here!"*

Not one stone (v. 2)—The only undisturbed parts of the temple following the Roman invasion of Jerusalem a few decades later in AD 70 were the huge foundation stones or footings of the edifice.

2 *And Jesus answered and said to him, "Do you see these great buildings? Not one stone shall be left upon another, that shall not be thrown down."*

3 *Now as He sat on the Mount of Olives opposite the temple, Peter, James, John, and Andrew asked Him privately,*

when will these things be (v. 4)—The disciples wrongly thought these events were at hand.

4 *"Tell us, when will these things be? And what will be the sign when all these things will be fulfilled?"*

the sign (v. 4)—The expectation was for a miraculous event (a bright light, darkness, an angelic visitation, etc.) to herald the coming of Christ's kingdom.

5 *And Jesus, answering them, began to say: "Take heed that no one deceives you.*

6 *For many will come in My name, saying, 'I am He,' and will deceive many.*

Take heed (v. 5)—literally, "see"; the idea is "keep your eyes open, beware"

7 *But when you hear of wars and rumors of wars, do not be troubled; for such things must happen, but the end is not yet.*

8 *For nation will rise against nation, and kingdom against kingdom. And there will be earthquakes in various places, and there will be famines and*

troubles. *These are the beginnings of sorrows.*

9 *"But watch out for yourselves, for they will deliver you up to councils, and you will be beaten in the synagogues. You will be brought before rulers and kings for My sake, for a testimony to them.*

10 *And the gospel must first be preached to all the nations.*

11 *But when they arrest you and deliver you up, do not worry beforehand, or premeditate what you will speak. But whatever is given you in that hour, speak that; for it is not you who speak, but the Holy Spirit.*

12 *Now brother will betray brother to death, and a father his child; and children will rise up against parents and cause them to be put to death.*

13 *And you will be hated by all for My name's sake. But he who endures to the end shall be saved.*

14 *"So when you see the 'abomination of desolation,' spoken of by Daniel the prophet, standing where it ought not" (let the reader understand), "then let those who are in Judea flee to the mountains.*

15 *Let him who is on the housetop not go down into the house, nor enter to take anything out of his house.*

16 *And let him who is in the field not go back to get his clothes.*

17 *But woe to those who are pregnant and to those who are nursing babies in those days!*

18 *And pray that your flight may not be in winter.*

19 *For in those days there will be tribulation, such as has not been since the beginning of the creation which God created until this time, nor ever shall be.*

20 *And unless the Lord had shortened those days, no flesh would be saved; but for the elect's sake, whom He chose, He shortened the days.*

21 *"Then if anyone says to you, 'Look, here is the Christ!' or, 'Look, He is there!' do not believe it.*

22 *For false christs and false prophets will rise and show signs and wonders to deceive, if possible, even the elect.*

the beginning of sorrows (v. 8)—The Greek word for "sorrows" means "birth pangs"; just as labor signals the end of pregnancy, so these signs and events would signal the end of the present age.

beaten (v. 9)—by local Jewish courts, usually with thirty-nine lashes so as not to violate Old Testament law

first be preached to all the nations (v. 10)—A worldwide proclamation of the gospel will precede God's final judgment.

for it is not you who speak (v. 11)—Persecuted believers can rely on the Holy Spirit for the words to say in defense of their faith in Christ.

endures to the end shall be saved (v. 13)—Endurance proves, not produces, salvation.

abomination of desolation (v. 14)—A historic event from the second century BC when Antiochus Epiphanes, king of Syria, sacrificed a pig on the temple altar; in the Tribulation, the Antichrist will also desecrate the altar by erecting an image of himself and demand it be worshiped.

(let the reader understand) (v. 14)—evidence that Jesus was not issuing these warnings to His own disciples but to a future generation of Christians

tribulation, such as has not been (v. 19)—an unparalleled time of pressure and anguish, yet future; the so-called Great Tribulation described further in the book of Revelation

the elect's sake (v. 20)—either the nation of Israel, or Gentile converts during the Tribulation

signs and wonders (v. 22)—Satanic inspired pseudo-miracles intended to elicit allegiance

23 *But take heed; see, I have told you all things beforehand.*

24 *"But in those days, after that tribulation, the sun will be darkened, and the moon will not give its light;*

25 *the stars of heaven will fall, and the powers in the heavens will be shaken.*

26 *Then they will see the Son of Man coming in the clouds with great power and glory.*

27 *And then He will send His angels, and gather together His elect from the four winds, from the farthest part of earth to the farthest part of heaven.*

28 *"Now learn this parable from the fig tree: When its branch has already become tender, and puts forth leaves, you know that summer is near.*

29 *So you also, when you see these things happening, know that it is near—at the doors!*

30 *Assuredly, I say to you, this generation will by no means pass away till all these things take place.*

31 *Heaven and earth will pass away, but My words will by no means pass away.*

32 *"But of that day and hour no one knows, not even the angels in heaven, nor the Son, but only the Father.*

33 *Take heed, watch and pray; for you do not know when the time is.*

34 *It is like a man going to a far country, who left his house and gave authority to his servants, and to each his work, and commanded the doorkeeper to watch.*

35 *Watch therefore, for you do not know when the master of the house is coming—in the evening, at midnight, at the crowing of the rooster, or in the morning—*

36 *lest, coming suddenly, he find you sleeping.*

37 *And what I say to you, I say to all: Watch!"*

1) According to Jesus, what worldwide events will happen during the Tribulation? What can followers of Christ during that time expect?

_____

_____

_____

2) How does Jesus describe His second coming in verses 24–27?

_____

_____

_____

3) In what way does the example of a fig tree help you understand what Jesus is saying about future events?

_____

_____

_____

GOING DEEPER

Matthew's account of the Olivet Discourse includes a more expanded explanation of Mark 13:34. Consider these added details in Matthew 24:44–51.

EXPLORING THE MEANING

4) What does this passage in Matthew suggest will be the results of an eager watchfulness to the promised return of Christ? Of a careless indifference?

_____

_____

_____

5) What do you think it means to "watch" for Jesus' return?

_____

_____

_____

6) Read 1 Thessalonians 5:1–11. What does this passage from the inspired pen of Paul add to your understanding of end-time events?

_____

_____

_____

7) Read 2 Peter 3:10–13. Given the certainty of the future events described in this passage and the others you've read, how should believers live in the present?

_____

_____

_____

TRUTH FOR TODAY

The theme of Christ's second coming permeates the New Testament and is the great anticipatory reality of Christian living. The Lord's return will be as real and as historical an event as His first coming. Believers look _back_ to the moment of saving faith in Christ when their souls were redeemed. They look _forward_ to the return of Christ when their bodies will be redeemed and they will enter into the promised fullness of salvation. In that day Satan will be defeated, the curse lifted, Christ worshiped, the creation liberated and restored, sin and death conquered, and the saints glorified.

REFLECTING ON THE TEXT

8) Do Jesus' words about the end times comfort you? Worry you? Explain your answers.

_____

_____

_____

9) What practical and specific steps can you take to live more consistently with eternity in view? What can you do this week to help those you love come to terms with their eternal futures?

_____

_____

_____

10) What specific questions do you still have about end-time events? Make it your goal this week to seek out answers (by talking to your pastor, personal study, etc.) to these questions.

_____

_____

_____

PERSONAL RESPONSE

Write out additional reflections, questions you may have, or a prayer.

_____

_____

_____

_____

_____

_____

_____

_____

_____

_____

_____

_____

_____

_____

_____

_____

_____

_____

ADDITIONAL NOTES

11

THE SERVANT IS WORSHIPED, BETRAYED, AND DENIED
Mark 14:1–72

DRAWING NEAR

When was the last time you truly felt God's presence and thanked Him for it? As you follow the events of Jesus' last days, take some time now to thank Him and worship Him.

_____

_____

_____

THE CONTEXT

In this fast-paced account of the life of Christ, events now become even more rapid-fire. Those who hate the Servant-Messiah sent from God begin moving quickly to destroy Him. Jesus' followers, perhaps sensing trouble, react with everything from worship to abandonment. Jesus uses every occasion to teach His disciples important truths they will need in the future.

As we enter Jesus' final week on earth, the events are filled with drama and emotion. Judas plans to betray Jesus, and the disciples make preparations for the Passover. Then Jesus struggles in prayer in Gethsemane for God's will to be done.

KEYS TO THE TEXT

The Jewish Feasts: The *Passover* was a very special feast day in Israel's religious calendar and was inextricably linked to what took place in the Exodus (Exod. 12–13). It became indelibly entrenched in Israel's tradition and has always marked the day of redemption from Egypt. Passover began with the slaying of the Passover lamb, which had to be a lamb without blemish. Friday of Passover would have begun on Thursday at sunset. According to Josephus, it was customary in his day to slay the lamb at about 3:00 PM. This was the time of day that Christ, the Christian's Passover lamb, died (1 Cor. 5:7; Luke 23:44–46). The *Feast of Unleavened Bread* began immediately after the Passover and commemorated the departure of the Israelites from Egypt (Exod. 23:15). Unleavened bread refers to the type of bread the Israelites were to take with them in their escape, which represented the absence of the leaven of sin in their lives and household.

UNLEASHING THE TEXT

Read 14:1–72, noting the key words and definitions next to the passage.

Mark 14:1–72 (NKJV)

Passover (v. 1)—a Jewish commemoration of the "passing over" of the homes of the Israelites by the angel of death just prior to the Exodus from Egypt

Feast of Unleavened Bread (v. 1)—a feast memorializing the Israelites' departure from Egypt

Not during the feast (v. 2)—The religious leaders did not wish to execute Christ when so many pilgrims (especially from Galilee) would be in the city and risk starting a riot.

And being in Bethany (v. 3)—Here Mark describes an event that actually had occurred the previous Saturday.

a woman (v. 3)—John 12:3 identifies this woman as Mary.

very costly . . . spikenard (vv. 3–5)—Pure nard, an exotic, imported oil sealed in a marble-like container; this costly substance (worth a year's wages) was likely Mary's most precious possession and her sacrificial act is a stunning example of love, devotion, and worship.

to anoint my body for burial (v. 8)—Probably without meaning to, the woman's act anticipated Jesus' death and entombment.

sought how he might conveniently (v. 11)—The idea is that he began looking for suitable occasion to carry out his dastardly plan.

1 After two days it was the Passover and the Feast of Unleavened Bread. And the chief priests and the scribes sought how they might take Him by trickery and put Him to death.

2 But they said, "Not during the feast, lest there be an uproar of the people."

3 And being in Bethany at the house of Simon the leper, as He sat at the table, a woman came having an alabaster flask of very costly oil of spikenard. Then she broke the flask and poured it on His head.

4 But there were some who were indignant among themselves, and said, "Why was this fragrant oil wasted?

5 For it might have been sold for more than three hundred denarii and given to the poor." And they criticized her sharply.

6 But Jesus said, "Let her alone. Why do you trouble her? She has done a good work for Me.

7 For you have the poor with you always, and whenever you wish you may do them good; but Me you do not have always.

8 She has done what she could. She has come beforehand to anoint My body for burial.

9 Assuredly, I say to you, wherever this gospel is preached in the whole world, what this woman has done will also be told as a memorial to her."

10 Then Judas Iscariot, one of the twelve, went to the chief priests to betray Him to them.

11 And when they heard it, they were glad, and promised to give him money. So he sought how he might conveniently betray Him.

12 *Now on the first day of Unleavened Bread, when they killed the Passover lamb, His disciples said to Him, "Where do You want us to go and prepare, that You may eat the Passover?"*

13 *And He sent out two of His disciples and said to them, "Go into the city, and a man will meet you carrying a pitcher of water; follow him.*

two of his disciples (v. 13)—Peter and John, according to Luke

14 *Wherever he goes in, say to the master of the house, 'The Teacher says, "Where is the guest room in which I may eat the Passover with My disciples?"'*

15 *Then he will show you a large upper room, furnished and prepared; there make ready for us."*

make ready (v. 15)—Peter and John had the responsibility of preparing the Passover meal.

16 *So His disciples went out, and came into the city, and found it just as He had said to them; and they prepared the Passover.*

17 *In the evening He came with the twelve.*

18 *Now as they sat and ate, Jesus said, "Assuredly, I say to you, one of you who eats with Me will betray Me."*

19 *And they began to be sorrowful, and to say to Him one by one, "Is it I?" And another said, "Is it I?"*

20 *He answered and said to them, "It is one of the twelve, who dips with Me in the dish.*

21 *The Son of Man indeed goes just as it is written of Him, but woe to that man by whom the Son of Man is betrayed! It would have been good for that man if he had never been born."*

The Son of Man . . . just as it is written (v. 21)—Christ was not a victim; His death was part of God's eternal plan and prophesied in the Old Testament.

22 *And as they were eating, Jesus took bread, blessed and broke it, and gave it to them and said, "Take, eat; this is My body."*

Jesus took bread . . . and said . . . "This is my body" (v. 22)—By this act, Christ transformed the Passover of the Old Testament into the New Covenant memorial of deliverance from sin.

23 *Then He took the cup, and when He had given thanks He gave it to them, and they all drank from it.*

24 *And He said to them, "This is My blood of the new covenant, which is shed for many.*

for many (v. 24)—that is, all who believe in Christ, both Jew and Gentile

25 *Assuredly, I say to you, I will no longer drink of the fruit of the vine until that day when I drink it new in the kingdom of God."*

26 *And when they had sung a hymn, they went out to the Mount of Olives.*

sung a hymn (v. 26)—probably Psalm 118, the traditional last psalm sung at the Passover

made to stumble (v. 27)—to fall away from loyalty to Christ, at least temporarily

27 Then Jesus said to them, "All of you will be made to stumble because of Me this night, for it is written: 'I will strike the Shepherd, And the sheep will be scattered.'

28 "But after I have been raised, I will go before you to Galilee."

29 Peter said to Him, "Even if all are made to stumble, yet I will not be."

30 Jesus said to him, "Assuredly, I say to you that today, even this night, before the rooster crows twice, you will deny Me three times."

31 But he spoke more vehemently, "If I have to die with You, I will not deny You!" And they all said likewise.

Gethsemane (v. 32)—a garden filled with olive trees on the slope of the Mount of Olives

32 Then they came to a place which was named Gethsemane; and He said to His disciples, "Sit here while I pray."

troubled (v. 33)—filled with terror or dread at the prospect of what was to come

33 And He took Peter, James, and John with Him, and He began to be troubled and deeply distressed.

34 Then He said to them, "My soul is exceedingly sorrowful, even to death. Stay here and watch."

35 He went a little farther, and fell on the ground, and prayed that if it were possible, the hour might pass from Him.

Abba (v. 36)—an intimate, endearing Aramaic word similar to the English "daddy"

nevertheless (v. 36)—Jesus was totally committed to doing the Father's will.

36 And He said, "Abba, Father, all things are possible for You. Take this cup away from Me; nevertheless, not what I will, but what You will."

37 Then He came and found them sleeping, and said to Peter, "Simon, are you sleeping? Could you not watch one hour?

38 Watch and pray, lest you enter into temptation. The spirit indeed is willing, but the flesh is weak."

the flesh is weak (v. 38)—Because willing spirits are still attached to unredeemed flesh, Christians struggle with doing right.

39 Again He went away and prayed, and spoke the same words.

40 And when He returned, He found them asleep again, for their eyes were heavy; and they did not know what to answer Him.

41 Then He came the third time and said to them, "Are you still sleeping and resting? It is enough! The hour has come; behold, the Son of Man is being betrayed into the hands of sinners.

42 *Rise, let us be going. See, My betrayer is at hand."*

43 *And immediately, while He was still speaking, Judas, one of the twelve, with a great multitude with swords and clubs, came from the chief priests and the scribes and the elders.*

44 *Now His betrayer had given them a signal, saying, "Whomever I kiss, He is the One; seize Him and lead Him away safely."*

kiss (v. 44)—an act depicting intimacy, respect, love, and affection, thus a despicable way of singling Christ out for arrest

45 *As soon as he had come, immediately he went up to Him and said to Him, "Rabbi, Rabbi!" and kissed Him.*

46 *Then they laid their hands on Him and took Him.*

47 *And one of those who stood by drew his sword and struck the servant of the high priest, and cut off his ear.*

one of those who stood by (v. 47)—identified by Luke and John as Peter

48 *Then Jesus answered and said to them, "Have you come out, as against a robber, with swords and clubs to take Me?*

49 *I was daily with you in the temple teaching, and you did not seize Me. But the Scriptures must be fulfilled."*

50 *Then they all forsook Him and fled.*

51 *Now a certain young man followed Him, having a linen cloth thrown around his naked body. And the young men laid hold of him,*

a certain young man (v. 51)—likely Mark himself

52 *and he left the linen cloth and fled from them naked.*

53 *And they led Jesus away to the high priest; and with him were assembled all the chief priests, the elders, and the scribes.*

54 *But Peter followed Him at a distance, right into the courtyard of the high priest. And he sat with the servants and warmed himself at the fire.*

55 *Now the chief priests and all the council sought testimony against Jesus to put Him to death, but found none.*

56 *For many bore false witness against Him, but their testimonies did not agree.*

many bore false witness against Him (v. 56)—There was no shortage of people to come forward at the Sanhedrin's invitation to consciously present false (and non-corroborating) testimony against the innocent Jesus.

57 *Then some rose up and bore false witness against Him, saying,*

58 *"We heard Him say, 'I will destroy this temple made with hands, and within three days I will build another made without hands.' "*

59 *But not even then did their testimony agree.*

60 *And the high priest stood up in the midst and asked Jesus, saying, "Do You answer nothing? What is it these men testify against You?"*

61 *But He kept silent and answered nothing. Again the high priest asked Him, saying to Him, "Are You the Christ, the Son of the Blessed?"*

62 *Jesus said, "I am. And you will see the Son of Man sitting at the right hand of the Power, and coming with the clouds of heaven."*

63 *Then the high priest tore his clothes and said, "What further need do we have of witnesses?*

64 *You have heard the blasphemy! What do you think?" And they all condemned Him to be deserving of death.*

65 *Then some began to spit on Him, and to blindfold Him, and to beat Him, and to say to Him, "Prophesy!" And the officers struck Him with the palms of their hands.*

66 *Now as Peter was below in the courtyard, one of the servant girls of the high priest came.*

67 *And when she saw Peter warming himself, she looked at him and said, "You also were with Jesus of Nazareth."*

68 *But he denied it, saying, "I neither know nor understand what you are saying." And he went out on the porch, and a rooster crowed.*

69 *And the servant girl saw him again, and began to say to those who stood by, "This is one of them."*

70 *But he denied it again. And a little later those who stood by said to Peter again, "Surely you are one of them; for you are a Galilean, and your speech shows it."*

71 *Then he began to curse and swear, "I do not know this Man of whom you speak!"*

72 *A second time the rooster crowed. Then Peter called to mind the word that Jesus had said to him, "Before the rooster crows twice, you will deny Me three times." And when he thought about it, he wept.*

he wept (v. 72)—The other Gospel writers add that Jesus looked Peter in the eye following the denial and that Peter wept bitterly.

1) What was the significance of Mary's anointing of Jesus?

_____

_____

_____

2) How did Judas and others view this extravagant display? How did Jesus view it?

_____

_____

_____

3) How does Mark describe Christ's mood in Gethsemane? What did Jesus suggest might result from the disciples' failure to pray?

_____

_____

_____

4) Describe the scene when the mob showed up to arrest Jesus. Why do you think Peter fought for Jesus one moment (v. 47) and fled the next (v. 50)?

_____

_____

_____

GOING DEEPER

Exodus 12:1–4 contains God's original instructions concerning the Jewish Passover celebration. Note the parallels between the Old Covenant and the New Covenant instituted in chapter 14 by the One whom John the Baptist called, "the Lamb of God who takes away the sin of the world" (John 1:29).

Exploring the Meaning

5) What parallels do you see between the original Passover celebration, Christ's sacrifice on the cross, and the Lord's Supper?

_____

_____

_____

6) Read 1 Corinthians 11:23–34. What additional instructions about the Lord's Supper does Paul give?

_____

_____

7) How did Jesus use prayer as a weapon against temptation? What else do you learn about Jesus from His words and actions in the Garden of Gethsemane?

_____

_____

_____

Truth for Today

Genuine worship is the supreme service a Christian can offer to Christ. There is a time for ministering to the poor, the sick, the naked, and the imprisoned. There is a time for witnessing to the lost and seeking to lead them to the Savior. There is a time for discipling new believers and helping them grow in the faith. There is a time for careful study and teaching of God's Word. But above all else what the Lord requires of His people is their true worship, without which everything else they may do in His name is empty and powerless.

Reflecting on the Text

8) How does Mary's example of costly worship motivate you? How can you emulate her example this week?

_____

_____

9) One of the lessons of this chapter surely must be, "let him who thinks he stands take heed lest he fall" (1 Corinthians 10:12). What warnings for your own life do you see in Peter's wretched denial of Christ?

_____

_____

_____

10) Jesus wrestled with God's will for His life, but willingly yielded to it. In what ways do you wrestle with God? How does Jesus' example help you?

_____

_____

_____

PERSONAL RESPONSE

Write out additional reflections, questions you may have, or a prayer.

_____

_____

_____

_____

_____

_____

_____

_____

_____

_____

_____

_____

ADDITIONAL NOTES

12

THE SERVANT CONQUERS SIN AND DEATH

Mark 15:1–16:20

DRAWING NEAR

What does it mean to you that Jesus went to the cross for *your* salvation?

_____

_____

_____

We serve a risen Savior! Relive the events of that first Easter weekend. Ask God to speak to you and transform you as you study this exciting passage.

THE CONTEXT

Mark closes his account with the two events that loom largest as far as the glory of God and the salvation of humankind are concerned: Jesus' crucifixion and resurrection. The crucifixion of Jesus Christ was the climax of redemptive history, the focal point of God's plan of salvation. God's redeeming work culminated in the cross, where the Lord Jesus bore the sins of the world. But the wickedness of human beings also reaches its apex. The death of Jesus Christ was the supreme revelation of the gracious love of God while also being the ultimate expression of the sinfulness of human beings.

The resurrection of Jesus Christ is the single greatest event in the history of the world. It is so foundational to Christianity that no one who denies it can be a true Christian. Without resurrection there is no Christian faith, no salvation, and no hope.

KEYS TO THE TEXT

Pilate: Jesus had two trials, one Jewish and religious, the other Roman and secular. Rome reserved the right of execution in capital cases, so Jesus had to be handed over to the Roman authorities for execution of the death sentence. Pilate's headquarters were in Caesarea, on the Mediterranean coast, but he was in Jerusalem for the Passover celebrations, so he oversaw the trial. Pilate could not afford another Jewish riot. The last riot had brought severe censure by Caesar himself. The mob was totally out of control, and it was clear that their only pacification would be Jesus' crucifixion. Pilate had never been known for mercy or diplomacy. Yet he did have a sense of justice. Had he been able to discover the least evidence that Jesus was guilty of a capital crime, he would have been greatly relieved and more than willing to grant His execution. But the fact that he unwaveringly maintained Jesus' innocence, rendering at least five public verdicts of not guilty, testifies to his inability to find any guilt in Him. He therefore repeatedly appealed to the Jewish leaders and to the multitudes to relinquish their demand for Jesus' death. But he was not courageous enough to risk his own welfare to protect Christ's life.

Atonement: The act by which God restores a relationship of harmony and unity between Himself and human beings. The word can be broken into three parts that express this great truth in simple but profound terms: "at-one-ment." Through God's atoning grace and forgiveness, we are reinstated to a relationship of at-one-ment with God, in spite of our sin. (*Nelson's New Illustrated Bible Dictionary*)

UNLEASHING THE TEXT

Read 15:1–16:20, noting the key words and definitions next to the passage.

Mark 15:1–16:20 (NKJV)

Pilate (v. 1)—Roman governor of Judea from AD 26–36

1 *Immediately, in the morning, the chief priests held a consultation with the elders and scribes and the whole council; and they bound Jesus, led Him away, and delivered Him to Pilate.*

"Are You the King of the Jews?" (v. 2)—The Jews' charge that Jesus claimed to be a king was of interest to Pilate because, if true, it would have made Christ guilty of treason against Rome.

2 *Then Pilate asked Him, "Are You the King of the Jews?" He answered and said to him, "It is as you say."*

3 *And the chief priests accused Him of many things, but He answered nothing.*

"Do you answer nothing?" (v. 4)—A silent prisoner not proclaiming his innocence was a rarity.

4 *Then Pilate asked Him again, saying, "Do You answer nothing? See how many things they testify against You!"*

5 *But Jesus still answered nothing, so that Pilate marveled.*

accustomed to releasing one prisoner (v. 6)—Pilate saw this Roman custom as a way out of the dilemma of having to pronounce guilt on an obviously innocent man.

6 *Now at the feast he was accustomed to releasing one prisoner to them, whomever they requested.*

Barabbas (v. 7)—a robber, according to John, and a murderer, according to Luke

7 *And there was one named Barabbas, who was chained with his fellow rebels; they had committed murder in the rebellion.*

8 *Then the multitude, crying aloud, began to ask him to do just as he had always done for them.*

9 *But Pilate answered them, saying, "Do you want me to release to you the King of the Jews?"*

10 *For he knew that the chief priests had handed Him over because of envy.*

11 *But the chief priests stirred up the crowd, so that he should rather release Barabbas to them.*

12 *Pilate answered and said to them again, "What then do you want me to do with Him whom you call the King of the Jews?"*

13 *So they cried out again, "Crucify Him!"*

14 *Then Pilate said to them, "Why, what evil has He done?" But they cried out all the more, "Crucify Him!"*

15 *So Pilate, wanting to gratify the crowd, released Barabbas to them; and he delivered Jesus, after he had scourged Him, to be crucified.*

scourged (v. 15)—beaten with a whip that featured metal or bone-tipped thongs

crucified (v. 15)—called by Roman writer Cicero "the cruelest and most hideous punishment possible"

16 *Then the soldiers led Him away into the hall called Praetorium, and they called together the whole garrison.*

17 *And they clothed Him with purple; and they twisted a crown of thorns, put it on His head,*

clothed Him with purple . . . crown of thorns (v. 17)—The callous and probably bored soldiers decided to hold a mock coronation of Jesus as the King of the Jews.

18 *and began to salute Him, "Hail, King of the Jews!"*

19 *Then they struck Him on the head with a reed and spat on Him; and bowing the knee, they worshiped Him.*

20 *And when they had mocked Him, they took the purple off Him, put His own clothes on Him, and led Him out to crucify Him.*

21 *Then they compelled a certain man, Simon a Cyrenian, the father of Alexander and Rufus, as he was coming out of the country and passing by, to bear His cross.*

22 *And they brought Him to the place Golgotha, which is translated, Place of a Skull.*

23 *Then they gave Him wine mingled with myrrh to drink, but He did not take it.*

wine mingled with myrrh (v. 23)—to temporarily deaden the pain and keep crucifixion victims from struggling excessively

24 *And when they crucified Him, they divided His garments, casting lots for them to determine what every man should take.*

third hour (v. 25)—9 AM based on the Jewish method of time-keeping

the inscription of His accusation (v. 26)—Typically, the condemned man's crime would be posted above his head.

wagging their heads (v. 29)— a gesture of contempt and derision

those who were crucified with Him (v. 32)—The two robbers joined in the reviling of Jesus, though one later repented.

darkness (v. 33) a mark of divine judgment, lasting from noon until 3 PM

Eloi . . . sabachthani (v. 34)— a quote of Psalm 22:1 in Aramaic, that Mark translates

cried out with a loud voice (v. 37)—an indication that Christ voluntarily gave up His life; it did not ebb away

the veil of the temple was torn in two (v. 38)—the massive curtain separating the Holy of Holies from the rest of the temple; a sign that the way into God's presence had been opened by the death of Christ

25 Now it was the third hour, and they crucified Him.

26 And the inscription of His accusation was written above: THE KING OF THE JEWS.

27 With Him they also crucified two robbers, one on His right and the other on His left.

28 So the Scripture was fulfilled which says, "And He was numbered with the transgressors."

29 And those who passed by blasphemed Him, wagging their heads and saying, "Aha! You who destroy the temple and build it in three days,

30 save Yourself, and come down from the cross!"

31 Likewise the chief priests also, mocking among themselves with the scribes, said, "He saved others; Himself He cannot save.

32 Let the Christ, the King of Israel, descend now from the cross, that we may see and believe." Even those who were crucified with Him reviled Him.

33 Now when the sixth hour had come, there was darkness over the whole land until the ninth hour.

34 And at the ninth hour Jesus cried out with a loud voice, saying, "Eloi, Eloi, lama sabachthani?" which is translated, "My God, My God, why have You forsaken Me?"

35 Some of those who stood by, when they heard that, said, "Look, He is calling for Elijah!"

36 Then someone ran and filled a sponge full of sour wine, put it on a reed, and offered it to Him to drink, saying, "Let Him alone; let us see if Elijah will come to take Him down."

37 And Jesus cried out with a loud voice, and breathed His last.

38 Then the veil of the temple was torn in two from top to bottom.

39 So when the centurion, who stood opposite Him, saw that He cried out like this and breathed His last, he said, "Truly this Man was the Son of God!"

40 There were also women looking on from afar, among whom were Mary Magdalene, Mary the mother of James the Less and of Joses, and Salome,

41 who also followed Him and ministered to Him when He was in Galilee, and many other women who came up with Him to Jerusalem.

42 Now when evening had come, because it was the Preparation Day, that is, the day before the Sabbath,

43 Joseph of Arimathea, a prominent council member, who was himself waiting for the kingdom of God, coming and taking courage, went in to Pilate and asked for the body of Jesus.

44 Pilate marveled that He was already dead; and summoning the centurion, he asked him if He had been dead for some time.

45 So when he found out from the centurion, he granted the body to Joseph.

46 Then he bought fine linen, took Him down, and wrapped Him in the linen. And he laid Him in a tomb which had been hewn out of the rock, and rolled a stone against the door of the tomb.

47 And Mary Magdalene and Mary the mother of Joses observed where He was laid.

16:1 Now when the Sabbath was past, Mary Magdalene, Mary the mother of James, and Salome bought spices, that they might come and anoint Him.

2 Very early in the morning, on the first day of the week, they came to the tomb when the sun had risen.

3 And they said among themselves, "Who will roll away the stone from the door of the tomb for us?"

4 But when they looked up, they saw that the stone had been rolled away—for it was very large.

5 And entering the tomb, they saw a young man clothed in a long white robe sitting on the right side; and they were alarmed.

6 But he said to them, "Do not be alarmed. You seek Jesus of Nazareth, who was crucified. He is risen! He is not here. See the place where they laid Him.

7 But go, tell His disciples—and Peter—that He is going before you into Galilee; there you will see Him, as He said to you."

many other women (vv. 40, 41)—In addition to Mary Magdalene, from whom Christ had cast out seven demons, Mary, the wife of Alphaeus and mother of James, and Salome, the wife of Zebedee and mother of James and John, a loyal group of women followed Jesus and helped support His ministry.

Joseph of Arimathea (v. 43)— a prominent member of the Sanhedrin who had opposed Jesus' condemnation

Pilate marveled (v. 44)— Crucifixion victims usually lingered in misery for days; thus, the governor was shocked to hear that Jesus was dead after only six hours.

wrapped Him in the linen (v. 46)—a perfumed burial cloth; Jews did not embalm corpses

when the Sabbath was past . . . in the morning, on the first day of the week (vv. 1–2)—Sunday morning

anoint (v. 1)—an act of love, using fragrant spices to offset the stench of death

the stone had been rolled away (v. 4)—not to let Jesus out, but to let witnesses in

a young man (v. 5)—an angel

—and Peter— (v. 7)—singled out because of his recent denial of Christ

afraid (v. 8)—overwhelmed by these mysterious events

Now when He rose . . . the accompanying signs. Amen (v. 9–20)—The external evidence strongly suggests that these verses were not originally part of Mark's Gospel. The earliest and most reliable manuscripts do not contain this passage. Perhaps a scribe or copyist added this ending some years later. Caution should be exercised in formulating doctrine solely from this passage.

8 *So they went out quickly and fled from the tomb, for they trembled and were amazed. And they said nothing to anyone, for they were afraid.*

9 *Now when He rose early on the first day of the week, He appeared first to Mary Magdalene, out of whom He had cast seven demons.*

10 *She went and told those who had been with Him, as they mourned and wept.*

11 *And when they heard that He was alive and had been seen by her, they did not believe.*

12 *After that, He appeared in another form to two of them as they walked and went into the country.*

13 *And they went and told it to the rest, but they did not believe them either.*

14 *Later He appeared to the eleven as they sat at the table; and He rebuked their unbelief and hardness of heart, because they did not believe those who had seen Him after He had risen.*

15 *And He said to them, "Go into all the world and preach the gospel to every creature.*

16 *He who believes and is baptized will be saved; but he who does not believe will be condemned.*

17 *And these signs will follow those who believe: In My name they will cast out demons; they will speak with new tongues;*

18 *they will take up serpents; and if they drink anything deadly, it will by no means hurt them; they will lay hands on the sick, and they will recover."*

19 *So then, after the Lord had spoken to them, He was received up into heaven, and sat down at the right hand of God.*

20 *And they went out and preached everywhere, the Lord working with them and confirming the word through the accompanying signs. Amen.*

1) The Jewish rulers had already tried Christ before the Sanhedrin (14:53–65). Now (chapter 15), Jesus is tried a second time before Pilate, the Roman governor. How were the two trials similar? How were they different?

_____

_____

_____

2) Mark's account of the crucifixion is not as detailed as the other Gospel writers. What key events did he record? How did the different witnesses of this event respond?

_____

_____

_____

3) Who was Joseph of Arimathea and why did he take charge of Jesus' body?

_____

_____

4) What part did the women play throughout these events?

_____

_____

_____

GOING DEEPER

Read the following passage from Isaiah 53:4–12 and consider its prophecy concerning the suffering willingly endured on our behalf by God's Servant.

EXPLORING THE MEANING

5) What added insights does Isaiah's ancient prophecy shed on the agonizing death of Christ for the sins of His people?

_____

_____

_____

6) Read the related passage in Luke 23:39–43. What strikes you about this conversation? What are the implications of Jesus' comments?

_____

_____

_____

7) Read John 20:11–39. What do these post-resurrection appearances by Christ mean for us?

_____

_____

_____

TRUTH FOR TODAY

God has been drawing, is now drawing, and, until the final judgment, will continue to draw sinful men and women back to Himself and to restore the world that sin has corrupted—all for the purpose of bringing glory to Himself. When sinners are saved, God is glorified because their salvation cost Him the death of His own Son, the immeasurable price that His magnanimous grace was willing to pay.

REFLECTING ON THE TEXT

8) How can you, in practical ways, show gratitude to God today for sending His Son Jesus to die on the cross for your sins?

_____

_____

_____

9) In what specific ways would today (or tomorrow) be different if you lived each moment with a conscious awareness of the fact that Jesus Christ is not only alive, but present with you?

_____

_____

_____

10) As you think back over this study of Mark, how has your understanding of Jesus as the Suffering Servant deepened? What have you learned? How has your faith been strengthened?

_____

_____

_____

PERSONAL RESPONSE

Write out additional reflections, questions you may have, or a prayer.

_____

_____

_____

_____

_____

_____

_____

_____

_____

_____

_____

_____

_____

_____

_____

_____

_____

_____

ADDITIONAL NOTES

Additional Notes

Additional Notes

Additional Notes

Additional Notes

Additional Notes

Look for these exciting titles by John MacArthur

Experiencing the Passion of Christ

Experiencing the Passion of Christ Student Edition

Twelve Extraordinary Women Workbook

Twelve Ordinary Men Workbook

Welcome to the Family:
What to Expect Now That You're a Christian

What the Bible Says About Parenting:
Biblical Principles for Raising Godly Children

Hard to Believe Workbook:
The High Cost and Infinite Value of Following Jesus

The John MacArthur Study Library for PDA

The MacArthur Bible Commentary

The MacArthur Study Bible, NKJV

The MacArthur Topical Bible, NKJV

The MacArthur Bible Commentary

The MacArthur Bible Handbook

The MacArthur Bible Studies series

Available at your local Christian Bookstore
or visit www.thomasnelson.com

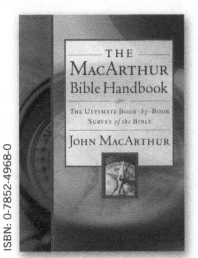